AF470295

A BEGINNER'S GUIDE TO PAINTING & DRAWING

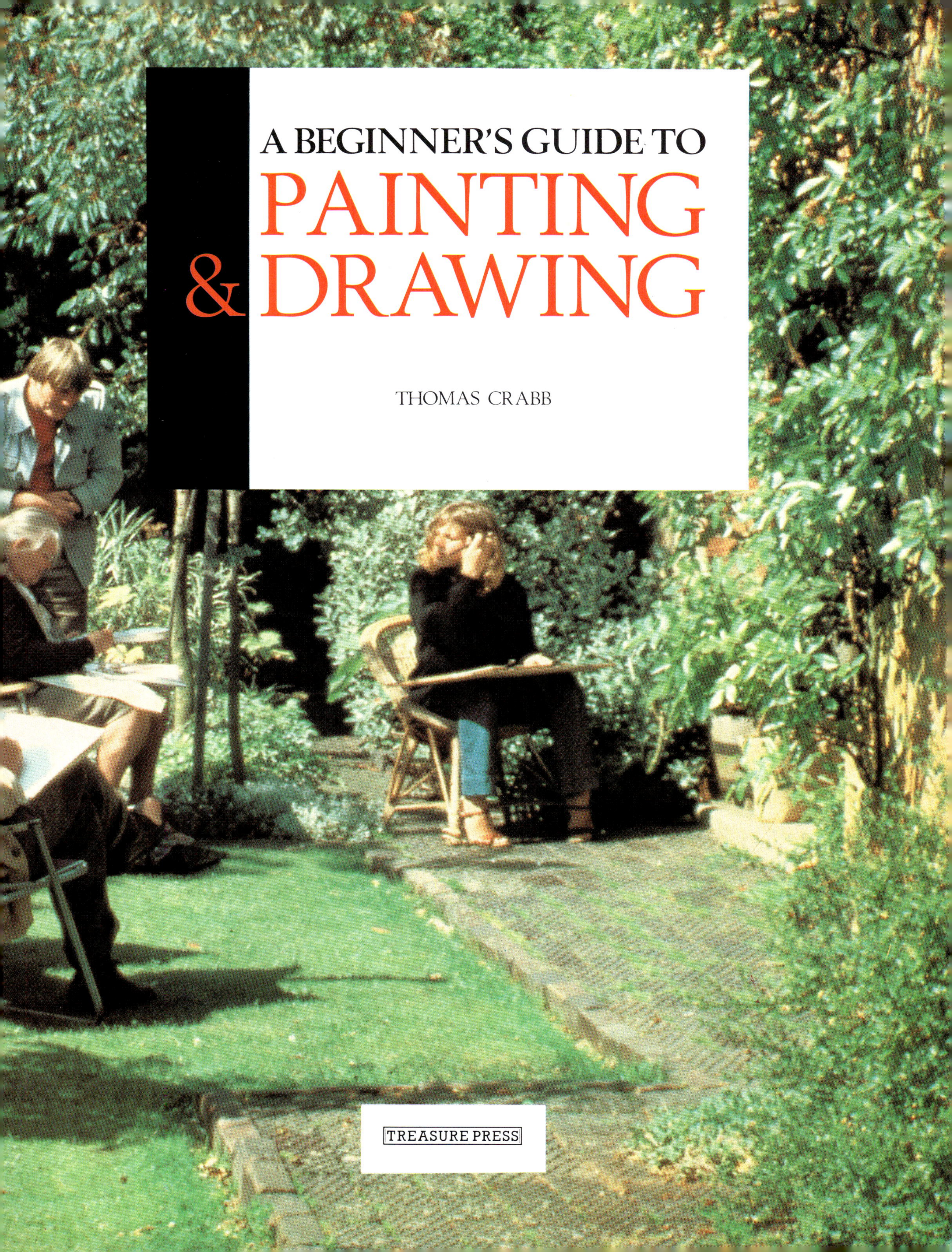

A BEGINNER'S GUIDE TO PAINTING & DRAWING

THOMAS CRABB

TREASURE PRESS

First published in Great Britain in 1981 by Park Lane Press under the title Painting and Drawing – A Beginner's Guide

This edition published in 1985 by
Treasure Press
Michelin House
81 Fulham Road
London SW3 6RB

Reprinted 1990

ISBN 1 85051 063 6

Printed by Mandarin Offset in Hong Kong

To Fred Packer of Central School of Art and Design for reading the manuscript, at every stage, and for his most constructive help and advice. Also to Jane Ginsborg who typed the manuscript innumerable times, clarifying my English at every stage

CONTENTS

INTERPRETATION

METHODS

SUBJECTS

INFORMATION

above: **Edouard Vuillard** (1868–1940)
THE MANTELPIECE oil on canvas
51.4 x 77.5 cm ($20\frac{1}{4}$ x $30\frac{1}{2}$ in)

This is a fine example of a still life. It is full of painterly and varied textural contrasts: the red pattern wallpaper, the fine delicate flowers of the cow parsley, the relatively flat area of cold hard marble and the soft towels on the clothes horse placed before the fire. They all work well together to form a whole.

page 1: *A final year Central School student at work. Around her are her exploratory pieces, each one contributing towards the painting on the easel. With such a large canvas it is essential for her to stand well back whilst applying pigment.*

title spread: *An outdoor session at the Barn Studio, Winslow, Bucks: a holiday and weekend centre that caters for artists of every level of experience.*

Painting and drawing

It can cost little and need no great expert knowledge to create pleasing works of art, modest or ambitious. Painting and drawing can be an intriguing way of passing time or a major obsession and way of life. But the dividing line between amateur and professional is almost impossible to draw. There have been gifted amateurs and untalented professionals. All of us have some kind of artistic ability and the only way to find out what kind we have is to 'have a go'. This book intends to help you do just that.

It is never too late to begin and one may paint and draw in a purpose-designed studio, in the wilds of the countryside or as an invalid confined to bed.

Visual arts enjoy, with swimming, the characteristic that one can exercise at the best pace to suit oneself at any particular moment. Regular exercise is, though, always the most desirable course.

The book is divided into three major sections. The first is on interpretation, and how far the imagination grows by what we see and experience around us in our daily lives. The second section is concerned with methods and the basic techniques of using different media such as oils, acrylics, watercolours and mixed media. The third section looks at some subjects that have excited artists over the last five hundred years. In addition to these sections, there are chapters about careers in art and design, going to evening classes and ways of finding a suitable course, exhibiting and showing work, and a comprehensive glossary of artists' terms.

This is a book that asks and encourages questions about why artists have wanted to and will, for the foreseeable future, want to paint and draw. Generally speaking creative people are much admired. It is some of this admiration that helps motivate the artist. We are all creative; many people need to know how to recognize and use their particular creative abilities, as well as being given guidance and help, so that they can produce visually pleasing drawings, paintings or sculpture.

Working with others

Every year in the late summer, many people consider attending evening or day classes in the fine arts: painting, drawing and sculpture. Some are naturally shy about their prospects and others are concerned about the commitment. Many feel they would like to try, and some are put off through fear that they lack talent or have too little knowledge of technical skills, and that this will stop them from being allowed to participate. With the aid of this book and with a certain amount of practical work, anyone should be able to walk into a painting studio with confidence.

No subject is any more difficult to depict than any other. It all depends on the person's interest in, knowledge of, and desire to be conversant with the subject. The human figure is thought by some to be the most difficult subject. This could well be because people believe they know when a drawing of a person or figure looks right and are less positive when looking at one of a flower or a tree. We are all familiar with the human body and have therefore a direct visual source of reference. But to the botanist, a drawing of a plant is easier to criticize than a drawing of a human figure.

All who wish to paint and draw must have enough confidence to show their work to others, and to carry out their painting studies in the presence of fellow artists. We all learn a great deal by watching others, receiving friendly advice and criticism, especially from those who are experiencing the same difficulties as ourselves. Sharing with others in a group, a class or in an exhibition provides mutual reinforcement and very great pleasure; it can also help us to sort out our own ideas.

The great explorers

The painter needs to be flexible in approach and to have an imaginative and inquiring mind. Great masters such as Leonardo and Michelangelo were also scientists and seekers after knowledge. Through painting and drawing they investigated their world and made discoveries in optics, anatomy, wave motion, etc. while other methods of inquiry at that time were based on religion and philosophy rather than observation.

Sometimes, while watching painters at work, it is quite easy to believe they are not thinking. They just seem to be covering the surface with paint, hardly ever stopping to judge the effect. These artists are often the first to deny that pictorial analysis and deliberate structure are necessary. They might even say that painting is not a learned occupation and play down the 'intellectual' side of their work. This is probably a subconscious feeling directed against the attempt by some people to explain everything by words and labels. Such artists believe that what they are doing is intelligent and rational. But their thinking about the subject is fully digested before they start the piece of work and is used almost automatically or subconsciously. While painting, and through manipulating physical materials, they are

left: **Rembrandt van Rijn** (1606–1689) *WOMAN WITH EARRINGS* oil on canvas 39.5 x 32.5 cm ($15\frac{1}{2}$ x $12\frac{3}{4}$ in)

An animated portrait of a woman trying on an earring. She has been caught at a moment of stillness in her excitement. Rembrandt, the master, fills in the shadowed side of the face with reflected light. No detail has been included that does not enhance the swirling composition All movement is towards her hands and the earring. Executed in browns, over the top of a monochrome painting, it emphasizes the warm colour of the oil light as well as picking up the colour of her lightly flushed skin.

continuing to inquire about things and ideas. At the same time they are using past knowledge stored in the mind, knowing instinctively what is going to happen in circumstances they have previously met. They have over the years developed a storehouse of knowledge and the memory of images, and this makes it possible for a fresh sequence of ideas to be triggered off as they work.

The art of patience

The artist watches and observes, often for a considerable time, allowing his visual interest in the subject to grow. He may make notes or marks in a sketchbook, or just contemplate. Then he will start a new work, adding the knowledge he has gathered over the years about colour, form and media to his present visual excitement.

Minutes or hours later the work has become a rounded whole. During the whole process, the painter has been storing further questions and findings in his memory, ready for the next occasion. This he will not wait for, but will conscientiously seek out and confront not waiting for inspiration.

It is sometimes tempting for beginners to follow this system of working. However, this seemingly direct but 'unthinking' approach will usually produce an unconvincing piece of work. On the other hand, thinking too hard while painting can produce stale and overworked results. It is difficult to find the perfect balance; one is on a tightrope between thought and pure gut reaction. The pleasure comes when all the thinking, struggling and experimenting come together at the same time, and then suddenly the last work in a series of paintings seems to be effortless. Probably before this happens again, there will be another series of rather more laborious paintings to be done, but eventually there will be another work in which we can take pleasure in our achievement.

WHY do artists paint and draw?

Artists express ideas through an activity, usually that of painting and drawing. In the process they produce something that can be looked at, and often raises questions in the spectator's mind. Few artists work with the sole intention of producing works of art. They are more often concerned with showing their understanding of some aspect of life. The artist is always making marks as his means of exploring and investigating. Instead of just fantasizing, he gives visual reality to the world of his imagination.

The language of painting and drawing is like other languages in that it is learned by doing, in the company of others. It can, and should, be strengthened by visits to art galleries and museums, as long as this is done in conjunction with the actual practice of painting and drawing. Creativity is difficult to define, and all too often self-expression is mistaken for it. Each one of us makes his individual contribution to whatever he does, be it accountancy, housekeeping or typing. All these can be, to a greater or lesser degree, creative and self-fulfilling, if a new or personal element is brought into the work.

Things that might trigger off ideas

Artists can be found in every type of occupation: they can be policemen, teachers, housewives, refuse collectors, lawyers or doctors. Not only do they think and perceive visually, but they have a particular interest which they may wish to pursue through painting or drawing. Art can be a means of communication with others, but it is also a way for the artist to find out what he feels and believes.

Although the experience gained through following a career can often provide a background well worth visual study, it is not necessary to have a profession to find reasons for painting and drawing. A curiosity about flowers, landscapes, bees, people or just shapes can be the trigger to start people painting or drawing.

Sometimes while handling a particular medium, such as Indian ink, images are made that startle and excite. This leads the artist into looking into the possibilities of the medium further.

An interest in media can be an absorbing obsession. The painter, once he has mastered some basic techniques, can quite easily be caught up in the magic of what the medium will allow him to create. He then finds subjects that fit into the knowledge he has acquired of the medium.

above: **Vincent van Gogh** (1853–1890)
PEASANT TILLING THE SOIL
black chalk and watercolour
62 x 47 cm (24⅜ x 18½ in)

A drawing that is the result of hours of observation. Van Gogh expresses clearly how the peasant's legs are spread awkwardly across a trench and the clumsy way in which the spade is being used. The direction of each mark helps to describe the form.

Accumulating images

Each piece of work an artist produces becomes a stepping stone to another line of inquiry. Few artists are totally

above: **John Constable** (1776–1837)
HARWICH SEA AND LIGHTHOUSE oil on canvas
31 x 49 cm ($12\frac{1}{4}$ x $19\frac{1}{2}$ in)

Constable's purpose was to depict the quiet quality of the evening light over the sea, and the way clouds catch the last glow of the setting sun. The horizon is gently brought to our attention by the sails of the tall ships. Great depth is achieved through the fine use of tonal values. The land looks sea-swept and desolate. He cleverly invites the viewer to walk with the man on the sea-front out of the shadow up to the houses which are partially obscured from our view.

happy with what they make, and most, while engaged on a painting or drawing, discover further questions to be answered about both medium and subject.

A deep trap the beginner can easily fall into is the desire to paint the image nestling in the back of the mind's eye. The danger is that by copying these mental images all questioning stops. Images that are preconceived and then copied are usually sterile and dead like passport photographs taken in impersonal automatic booths. The true visual artist, painter or photographer, enjoys watching and absorbing knowledge, then refining it until only the essential ingredients are left. The reproduction of the image held in the mind's eye does not allow for any further developments to take place as the painting takes shape.

Distilling information from detail

An important part of the artist's abilities is learning how to collect information, as without it visual results can often be wishy-washy. It has to be sifted and sorted; this is something that happens both consciously and subconsciously. Artists sometimes find that one of the best ways of doing this is to make jottings on paper or canvas, relating their visual impact to each other as they are made. Only when actual images have been made can they be challenged. They can also, at this stage, be related by the artists to past images seen or made.

Students often pay unnecessary attention to minute particulars or detail, in the mistaken belief that they are providing information. Detail is no substitute for intention. It merely distracts the viewer. Deciding what to leave out can be painfully difficult, especially when the artist is unsure of the purpose of the drawing. On the other hand, it is perfectly reasonable to include excess information in the first draft and subsequently, in later drawings, eliminate it as superfluous.

The artist paints or draws because he cannot ignore his need to peel back and examine the layers of reality that he perceives. He has continually to ask questions about his materials, media and subject matter.

The artist, then, thinks through doing, learns through making, discovers through creating and expresses through activity; he cannot be passive.

Ways of SEEING

When we are born, our eyes and optic system are physically fairly well developed. After about two weeks, children can make their eyes focus and follow moving objects. They are aware of sound, light and touch, without any ability to link them. Through the use of hands, lips and ears, they learn to connect the patterns they see with objects. Later these are identifiable by name. Sadly, some people are not taught to develop their visual perception much beyond this stage.

Seeing is closely connected with perception, that is, the ability to understand and comprehend the world through the senses. Human beings, in comparison with animals, take a long time to reach adulthood, but while doing so develop a wide range of abilities and skills. The hawk may be able to see tiny animals on the ground hundreds of feet below, for its senses have evolved in such a way as to be able to spot food and danger. We, however, lead much more complicated lives than animals and we have to do more with our eyes than seek food.

Strengthening our senses

Seeing is just one of our senses, the eye being a highly developed instrument able to perform functions that as yet no camera can. Because we have such a marvellous device as the eye, some of our other sense organs do not work as hard or as well as they might. A blind man, so I am told, can smell danger, while the sighted search for it with their eyes. The person who cannot smell can still appreciate much about food: its physical texture, its colour and its shape. No sense organ can truly be said to be working unless it is operating in conjunction with the others. With music, we cannot see the sounds, but it can conjure up visual memories. We have all had a different kind of home life, schooling and working environment. Each one of us experiences the world in a way that is radically different in some respects from the experience of others. We all see things differently. Advertising and marketing people spend much time and energy trying to discover what we all have in common in order to discover what products and services we might be persuaded to buy in quantity.

Abandoning past experience

Every day each of us gains new experiences that cause us to change our minds about the kinds of products or services we want. It follows that the same ought to be true in the manner we see objects. We rarely see what we are looking at, as often we do not actually know what we are looking for.

Medical scientists are known to have mental 'blind spots' when examining specimens under the microscope. They can let pass under their eyes what they are not

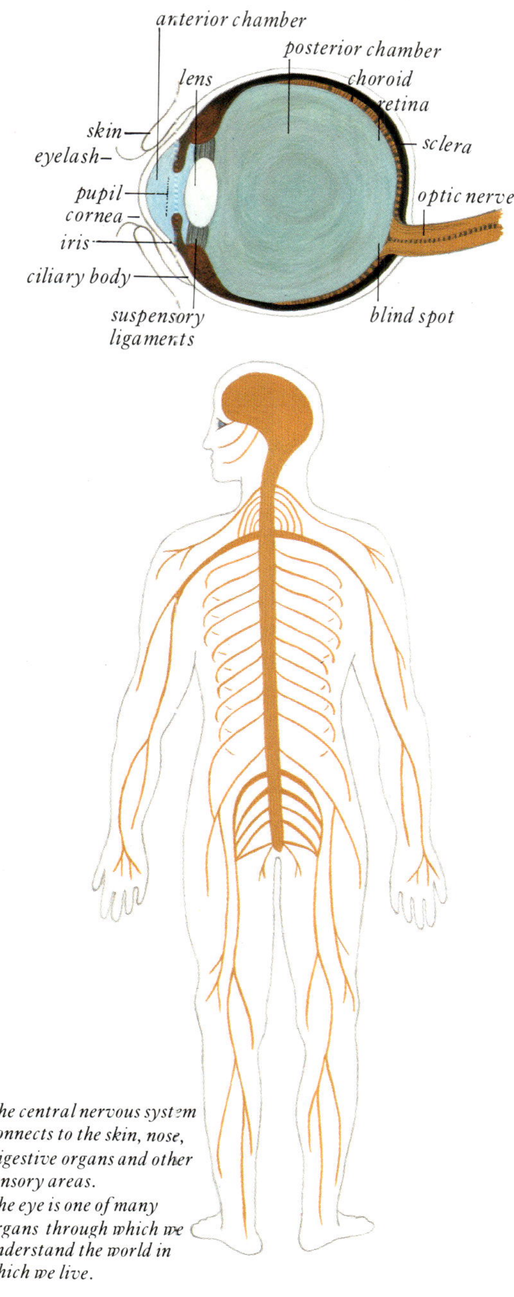

The central nervous system connects to the skin, nose, digestive organs and other sensory areas. The eye is one of many organs through which we understand the world in which we live.

specifically looking for, or dismiss the unexpected. The matter they dismiss or overlook may be the cause of an illness, or significant in some other way.

The artist might be likened to an expert on engines. If we were to take a ride in a car with an experienced engineer he might be able to tell us a great deal about the condition of the engine from just listening and feeling any vibrations. Noises are like pictures or words to the expert mechanic. The more knowledgeable the artist, the greater the variety of different shades that can be observed in what he sees around him.

The camera as a recorder

Students are sometimes told on arrival at art school that they are now going to have to unlearn everything they have previously been taught about art. This rightly disturbs the more mature student, who cannot understand why he should disregard acquired experience. Some of the less mature are happier, since they fear being given too much guidance and instruction, believing that it might stop them from being creative. They suspect that the imagination can be dulled by being given too much information. By gaining technical expertise, they believe they will become practitioners of

above: **Josef Albers** (1888–1976)
HOMAGE TO THE SQUARE
oil on hardboard 76.2 x 76.2 cm (30 x 30 in)

Colours tend to become more powerful as they are watched. The fiery centre glows, causing the eye to move in and out of the picture's space, hovering without a firm resting place.

below: *Magazines on this newspaper stand show a wide range of visual tastes*

René Magritte
(1898–1967)
NOT TO BE REPRODUCED
oil on canvas
32.5 x 26.5 cm ($12\frac{3}{4}$ x $10\frac{1}{2}$ in)

The unexpected, a realism without truth. While the reflection of the man is impossible, that of the book is realistic. A visual statement that keeps the viewer looking and checking his own sense of reality. Maybe the picture will change and all will be as normal. The contradictory humour of the title is typical of the Surrealists' literary bias. In their case the title is often an important ingredient in the work's impact.

Grandma Moses
(1860–1954)
WHITE CHRISTMAS
oil on hardboard
60.5 x 50 cm ($23\frac{3}{4}$ x $19\frac{3}{4}$ in)

A direct and in many ways charming picture. It is viewed with an eye that sees in a similar way to the painters of the Far East, who present distance by laying it out flat before them. The painting is full of movement. The composition leads us nowhere and is evidence of piecemeal putting together of visual images. This is all emphasized by the scale of the people, some too large and some impossibly small. The sky which could be a restful haven stands out as an isolated patch of blue. The painting's charm lies in its naïvety.

methods rather than of creative ideas. This is untrue, because the imagination is only as strong as the depths of experience acquired by the person. It is also of little use to have marvellous ideas without the desire, and the ability too, to carry them through. Both these aspects of art can be reinforced by looking at the work of other people, especially the famous and radical among our contemporaries. By appreciating a little of what motivates them and how they go about clearing away their own mists of ignorance, we can be happier using our own flights of fantasy. We all have day dreams, but we are inclined to discount them through a lack of confidence, and sometimes for fear of being laughed at.

Reality and fantasy are never far apart. When as children we opened our eyes in the middle of the night and imagined the shadows on the ceiling to be spirits wandering around us, we were using our limited past experience to build up a picture. We were seeing with our imagination things we felt were real, and at the same time, we felt we should disregard them, knowing they were only shadows, no matter how frightening. The situation of seeing was real, but it was fantasies we saw.

Psychology runs wild

The Surrealists are probably the most famous group of people who made images, words and sounds from the exploitation of the subconscious. They were fascinated by the work of the psychologist Freud who taught about the frustrations of the subconscious. He explained what damage could occur if people denied their fantasies some form of harmless outlet. The Surrealists devised ways of reaching into the subconscious through games such as automatic writing. Their visual work often had a literary slant; for instance, there would be a discrepancy between the title of a picture and its content. Visual equivalents to figures of speech were found, such as visual puns, mixed metaphors and double meanings. The purpose was in general to shock us out of complacency and our concepts of what is right, proper or acceptable. Sometimes the works would touch a raw nerve by dealing with matters about which we are usually reticent: sex, death, mutilation, the images of our dreams and repressed desires. Disturbing images were produced from such anomalies as a telephone sitting on an omelette, limp watches, fur-lined teacups and a urinal signed as a work of art. There was of course a serious purpose in these disturbing images, shocking to many at the time. The artists were seeing afresh familiar things and communicating the excitement this produced.

Being prepared to look

Since the advent of photography, it is sometimes said by photographers that portraiture as a branch of painting must surely be limited in its appeal to both artist and sitter. They say that the camera can see and record much more exactly than the artist, and in the hands of a capable photographer can do an equally good job of flattery. This is surely not so. The human brain sees with the aid of two eyes, and has the ability to select the picture area as well as filter out anything that is not important to the viewer. The eye is also able to see a greater range of tones and colour than any film made. Sometimes it needs to adapt to lighting conditions, which it does well as it is a very sensitive instrument. A camera is a mechanical device that needs the eye to show it what part of the image is to be selected. Then it will record, via the use of the lens. The camera has not the automatic advantage that the artist has of perceiving three-dimensional form and being able to interpret what is seen directly on to a flat surface. Seeing and recording through the lens can be a useful form of note taking; it is not, however, a substitute for the analytical nature of drawing. This can be demonstrated: if one tries to make a painting from the information given in a photograph or series of photographs, rather than from life or drawings, one realizes how much necessary information is missing in the photographs.

Uncovering what we see

We can learn how to see clearly by continually trying to capture in a visual form what we encounter. By drawing, we peel back the layers of obscurity to reveal the underlying nature of the object or experience leading to an understanding and knowledge which we store in our memory. Such investigation through observation gives us our future points of reference. Later we are able to go back and relate what we saw then with what we are seeing now. Painting is just one way of using a visual language, and the essence of any language is that it should communicate, even if this, in the case of painting, is only with ourselves. For fairly obvious reasons, we desire to paint what we see in front of us in a way that is as close as can be to the real object or person. This is of course impossible, even if we allow for the fact that we do not really expect to put the actual situation on to the canvas. All we can do is to represent one aspect of that situation extracting the key elements and reinforcing the image with information from our memory store. The character that we are trying to communicate might simply be in the colour. All the marks we make will aim to describe and accentuate this colour quality. As the painting proceeds, we will probably see more and will have to select even more stringently.

A game for the very young is putting blocks into a variety of holes. At first the child will have no discrimination. Square blocks will be tried in round holes. Then experience and memory will take over, and the child will learn to see which holes match which blocks. He will do this through trial and error. The artist does the same, placing for instance one patch of colour next to another, seeing the visual result and mentally recording the results of their reaction. This bank of stored memories of visual effects will be drawn on later, when required for another painting or drawing.

Working with LIGHT

On waking up after a night's sleep we are immediately aware of the amount of light filling the space in our rooms. A dark room my tell us that the sky is grey and overcast. A brightly lit room on a midwinter morning may be a signal to us that snow has fallen and that the day will be a crisp and cold one.

All this information depends on the part of the world we inhabit. British artists are fortunate that light conditions change so quickly, for the result is that they are able to see surface shapes changing colour and texture in the space of a few hours. This makes painting out of doors in Britain exciting and challenging. It is through the action of light that we are enabled to use our eyes; they confirm what other senses tell us is happening.

Drawing a sphere

The way light is reflected helps us to see things as solid. We see tonal changes on an object such as a ball which are common to all spheres. Often there is a strip of highlight along the shadow edge. This highlight has been reflected from the surface on which the sphere has been placed. It is this line of bright light that informs us that the object

1

2

left: **Edouard Manet**
(1832–1883)
THE HOUSE AT RUEIL
oil on canvas
89.5 x 71.7 cm ($35\frac{1}{4}$ x $28\frac{1}{4}$ in)

Creating mood can be all-important for the artist. Manet achieves this by depicting the sparkling sharp light of a summer's day combined with the comparatively cool colours of the shadowed area under the trees. He adds to this the light on the running water of the stream. All this contributes to giving the viewer a sense of peace and well being.

opposite: **Ramón Casas**
(1866–1932)
PARIS LANDSCAPE
oil on canvas
51 x 66 cm (20 x 26 in)
This painting of the Moulin de la Galette garden in the evening light of Paris breathes romance. The artist makes the girl the focus of interest by placing her near the centre, and letting the light play gently on her pale-coloured hat as well as the table-cloth and scarf. Darker fabrics would have made her fade into the background, as they do the man in the shadows near the gate. Only his white collar brings him to our attention.

4

5

Observing light

1 *The source of light in this picture is even and overhead. Shapes are clearly defined, though the objects appear to be floating*
2 *With back lighting the result is often romantic. Shapes and surfaces are soft and unclear.*
3 *Harsh directed light makes objects appear hard.*
4 *A single gentle light like the evening sun gives a feeling of clarity without great detail*
5 *This moonlight effect hides a fair amount of information*

above left: **Georges Seurat** (1859–1891)
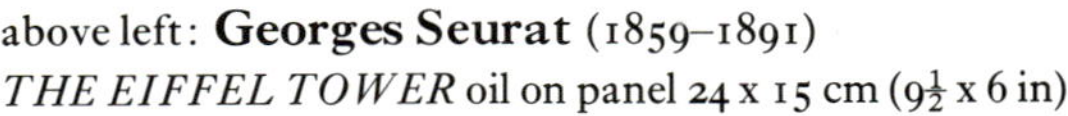
THE EIFFEL TOWER oil on panel 24 x 15 cm (9½ x 6 in)

Painted in dots over a near-white primed surface. This way of using pigment makes the hues vibrate and shimmer as if in strong sunlight. The top of the tower is left unpainted so as to appear hidden in cloud.

above right: **Gerard Dou** (1613–1675)
OLD WOMAN READING oil on canvas
71 x 55.5 cm (28 x 21⅞ in)

At first this work appears to be concerned with detail; it is, though, a painting about the way light picks up texture as well as how reflected light softens what might have been hard shadows.

is spherical and not flat. Also some light from the sphere is reflected back into the shadow cast by the sphere.

One of the strangest things about light is that we are not aware of its existence until it is reflected. A good example of this can be seen in the cinema. The projector throws a light at the screen which reflects the result, the picture. At the start of the day's viewing, the atmosphere is clear of cigarette smoke. Later, as smoke fills the air, the projection beam becomes obvious. The smoke particles interrupt the flow of light onto the screen.

The degree of surface light in painting and drawing is called tone. It is a useful idea to decide on a tonal range for the work before we begin to paint or draw. Some of the alternatives we have are: 1 to use extremes of black and white with no tonal changes in between. 2 to use the lighter end of the tonal scale, picking out only some parts which are to be very dark in order to give contrast and emphasis to the light areas. 3 to use the darker end of the tonal scale, again picking out some parts in near-white, to give a tonal contrast. 4 trying to use the whole range of tones possible, again deciding at the beginning which will be the darker tones and which the lightest, and which will be in the middle.

A useful aid

One device that will aid the less experienced artist is a tonal chart. To make it, divide a strip of paper 7in by 1in into 1in squares. Number the squares 1 to 7. Paint the first square white and the last one black. Paint the middle square (no 4) mid-grey; now paint 2 and 3 and 5 and 6 in even steps between mid-grey and black. Make sure that each tone is half-way between its neighbours. This scale can be used to decide between one tonal value and another. It is possible to note the tone values on a

above: **Ignacio Mallol** (1892–1940)
ROSE TREES/COSTA BRAVA oil on canvas
110 x 99 cm ($43\frac{3}{8}$ x 39 in)

Instead of cast shadows in this painting there are cast patches of light. They fall like large raindrops on a bright summer's day. This is a high key painting; all the tonal differences are subdued, with rare touches of near-black around the model boat. The colours are muted tints. They strengthen our feeling of constant heat from which the rose trees give little shade. Between the branches it is possible to see how the 'background' was painted in over the structure of the tree. This is a useful way of making space appear to be smothered by light, as seen through fine tracery.

drawing from nature by these numbers, and then make a painting from this information when back in the studio.

The difference between two tones is called contrast. To achieve this it is not necessary to have great differences; it is only necessary to have a clearly defined boundary at the place the two tones meet. The technical name for this is acutance.

The painter or draughtsman has a distinct advantage over the photographer in his ability to use light. The artist can search in the shadows and tease out information. He can also look into the areas of bright light and paint the minute differences the lens of a camera cannot see nor be so selective in finding. Also, the lens that has been tuned to see the differences at one end of the tonal range is completely unable to differentiate tones at the other end. The camera can only be adjusted to record a very limited tonal range.

Light can be either a cruel or a loving medium to work with. Used so that it shines across the skin, it shows up every bump and wrinkle. It can be kind and warm when it is reflected, soft without intensity.

Scattered light, which is not intense in its brightness, can reveal details most clearly. Because the eye does not have to strain looking into shadows or squint at bright light, detail is easily discernible. Soft and subtle textures can be seen. Colours become bright and intense for they are neither overlit and therefore washed out, nor underlit and subdued.

Most people respond to colour. Modern personality tests include the use of colour as a basis for their conclusions. Tibetan priests and Eastern philosophers teach that each one of us is physically surrounded by colour which describes our personality. It is believed that everyone who practises hard can witness these colours themselves.

Colours can be used expressively, symbolically or impressionistically. Colour has emotive force. Cool colours express recession and distance; warm colours advance and are associated with aggression. 'The blues' as used by jazz and soul singers implies feelings of distance, loneliness and sadness.

There are no absolute rules for using colour, and it is not essential to know all about colour theory. It is more important to practise using colour and to be sensitive to its effects. It is not enough just to study reproductions; whenever possible see how other people use colour, through art galleries, art schools, outdoor exhibitions or a visit to a friend's studio.

Remembering colours

Most people have a poor colour memory. The naming of colours depends substantially on the association of ideas. There are, for instance, Bantu peoples in southern Africa with more than 26 terms to designate the different colours of their cattle.

Make-up is one way of using colour that some girls become very skilled at. They learn that reddish skin can be subdued by a judicious use of green foundation, that the right blue eyeshadow can give brown eyes a deeper and more mysterious appearance. A face that is thought to be too long or round can be altered quickly with the correct kind of colour application. All this knowledge is learned through the desire to be attractive in a particular way. A curiosity and interest in colour has strengthened the ability to make use of these discoveries.

What is colour and how does it come about? Energy from the sun reaches us in the form of light. As it hits the particles in the earth's atmosphere, it becomes visible. These rays of white light contain bands of each of the 'spectral' colours. (Raindrops can act as a prism and separate these out into the separate colours of the

above: **James McNeill Whistler** (1837–1903)
SYMPHONY IN WHITE NO. 3 oil on canvas
51.4 x 76.5 cm (20¼ x 30⅛ in)

This delicate and textural painting shows how whites can be used positively. Each tint of white becomes a colour, together combining to produce a delicate harmony.

opposite: **Auguste Renoir** (1841–1919)
ON THE TERRACE oil on canvas 100.3 x 81 cm (39½ x 32in) (detail)

This artist uses a sparkling palette that is never allowed to go muddy by overmixing. Soft, smooth skin tones blend well with the brilliance of the millinery. The viewer may possibly be able to feel the texture of the silk next to the skin.

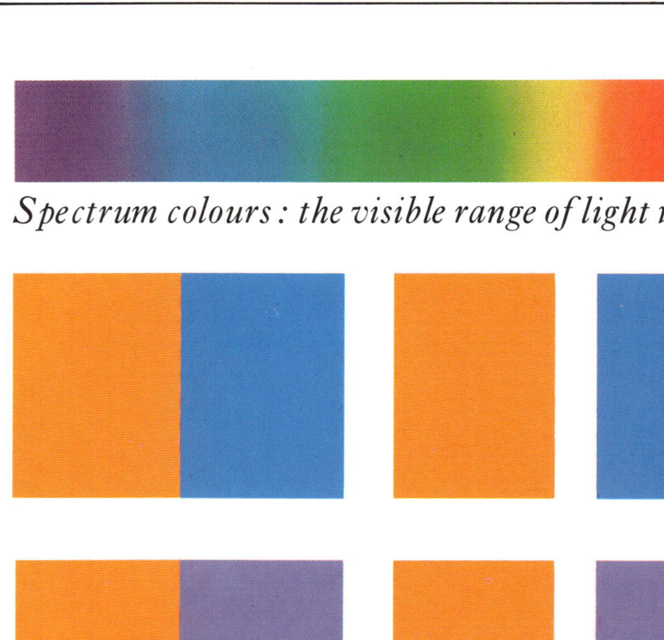

Spectrum colours: the visible range of light waves.

The top two areas are contrasting colours (as far as is possible when printing). The joining border should vibrate. The bottom two areas are colours which are similar but not contrasting. The joining border should not vibrate.

The top two colours are the same as those on the left, with a band of white between them.
The bottom two colours are again a repeat of those on their right. The colours in the top areas, should, as they are contrasting, enhance each other.

The colours in the top square are additive, mixing together to show white. The colours in the bottom square are subtractive, mixing together to show black. They reflect no light when mixed.

rainbow.) When white light strikes an object, that object reflects back part of the light and absorbs part as energy or heat. We see the part that is reflected as a colour. A green ball absorbs all the colours of the spectrum except green, which it rejects. The green light is bounced back to us so we are aware of a green object. Strictly speaking, the object is 'anti-green'. Those objects that will not absorb any part of the colour spectrum appear to us to be white. Subtle changes in the surface colour of objects occur when, say, the surface is covered with microscopically small particles or facets that reflect different parts of the spectrum.

Nature's way of mixing colour

Colours are mixed either additively or subtractively. Colours made with projected light are additive. Projected red, blue and yellow light combine to make white light. A red beam of light is projected onto a white screen. On the now red screen, a green light is projected and the screen appears yellow. When a blue light is added, the result is a totally white reflection. This is additive mixing, for together these lights make white. The primary colours of light are red, green and blue.

Subtractive mixing is when colours mixed together absorb white light, as when mixing pigment. A red pigment mixed with its complementary, green, makes black. The green absorbs all the colours of the light spectrum except green, and the red absorbs that, leaving no part of the spectrum to be reflected. This is a subtle way of mixing a black, often preferable to using black

above: **Paul Gauguin** (1848–1903)
GIRL WITH FRUIT oil on canvas 92 x 73 cm ($36\frac{1}{4}$ x $28\frac{3}{4}$ in)

Luminous colour created through careful feeling for tonal values. A painting that could only be achieved after considerable experience. Firmly and positively applied oil paint, saturated colour with a nice sense of harmony together with discords in the qualities of line.

opposite below: **Henri Matisse** (1869–1954)
STILL LIFE oil on canvas 66 x 81 cm (26 x $31\frac{7}{8}$ in)

Painted as if every area of colour were isolated, but no shape is painted without visual reference to its neighbour. A painterly painting for it relies on colour and shape rather than line. The perspective of the shapes is true; they were seen at the time both separately and as a whole.

pigment. The three primary pigment colours are yellow, magenta and cyan (approximately yellow, red and blue).

Colour behaves in similar ways to sound in music. Colours can be pleasant together in the right context, yet unpleasant in another, so seeming discordant. Colours can oppose each other, yet work effectively in the painting as a whole. Complementary colours oppose each other—they do not necessarily clash. It is quite simple to see which colours oppose each other. Take a small piece of coloured paper and place it on one half of

a much larger piece of white paper. Quietly look at the colour without moving your eyes away from it for about half a minute. Transfer your gaze to the white area. After a few moments you will see a colour enclosed by a grey shape. This after-image colour is the exact opposite of that of the coloured paper. If the paper was a strong colour the after-image will appear thin, and it will also be of the opposite hue. The grey enclosure is the after-image of the white paper background.

An area of red placed next to its opposite, green, will vibrate where the colours join, producing the effect of a black line. As long as they are stared at, they will continue to reinforce each other, the red becoming redder and the green greener, and the line more intense. When moved apart, the result is less violent, and when placed in context and surrounded by other colours, they will reinforce and compositionally enhance each other. The Impressionists used the complementary colour of an object to create its shadow. They tried to use a limited range of pure colours, painted directly and unmixed on to the canvas, giving an impression of immediacy and light. The Pointillistes developed this effect of optical mixing. In their technique, separate dots of colour bounce back individual rays of light which are visually blended in the viewer's eye, combining the effect of additive and subtractive mixing.

Shadows contain colour

A red object has a certain amount of green light in its shadow. This is complicated by the fact that the red colour of the object reflects its colour into the shadow. The way we see the colour of an object depends on the colour of the object next to it. This is one of the reasons why it is inadvisable to paint individual objects in isolation, straight on to a white canvas. It is also why some painters cover their canvas in a warm brown tone over the pure white of the prepared surface.

Seventeenth-century painters found that by dragging a lightly loaded brush of light colour over an area of darker colour it appeared to have been painted a cool blue. This is called a turbid medium effect. The light, warm colour of the flesh produces a cool blue shadow when 'scumbled' in this way over dark under-painting. You can see this effect if you visit the National Gallery in London, as it is used by Rubens in his portrait of a girl in a straw hat.

When studying colour through the painting of still lives, portraiture or landscape, it is important to consider the colour of the source of light as well as the colour of the light used in the working environment. Only direct sunlight is white in Britain. Colours in the sky result from light having to pass through and reflect off particles in the earth's atmosphere. Evening light, for instance, is blue, and sunsets can produce a saturating red light. When sunlight comes from a low angle, as just before dusk, surface colours seem to increase in luminosity and subtlety: an effect for painters to look out for.

People who live in towns experience space in an entirely different way to those who live in the country. Being housed in small boxes and in tightly enclosed areas makes it inevitable that some feel uncomfortable and strange when surrounded by open countryside. This may explain the reluctance of some people to leave the enclosed space of their cars.

We are aware of many forms of space. Vacuum is one: total emptiness. Space is also a name given to matters and forces outside the earth's atmosphere, those vast areas of the unknown waiting to be explored. This interplanetary space is far from empty. All matter is made of molecules and atoms. Molecules, when enlarged, appear to consist mainly of large quantities of space in which one or more atoms are rushing around, the whole mass being held together by electro-magnetic forces. These atoms can subsequently be magnified to reveal a similar process happening on a smaller scale still. The earth in the solar system is a relatively small particle, kept in place by forces which are barely understood. Our solar system is yet another small part of a greater structure called the universe.

Always remember that nothing stands in isolation, but that all things have physical relationships to each other in reality, and the artist bears this in mind.

Transported through space

If one wishes to create great depth and space in a painting or drawing it is a help to imagine oneself in a tiny helicopter trying to fly around the space that is being defined on the flat surface. This sort of space is created through knowledge of the interrelationship of objects within it. Space in a painting is positive or active, playing an obviously important part in the subject of the work, or it can be passive and subtle, not intruding nor making its presence felt. This second type of pictorial space is often referred to as atmospheric, yet this does not adequately describe its effect. When we walk into a room we are consciously or unconsciously aware that it has its own atmosphere. We all know people who are so sensitive to the appearance of their own living space that they spend most of their creative energy making it bearable and pleasant to live in.

Vibrations

But what is it about this space or environment that gives us the impression we receive? Factors include the proportions of the room, its length, breadth and height, and the size, shape and position of the objects in the room. Without our realizing it, the placing of the objects 'articulates' the space. Over concern for detail in a painting or drawing can destroy its visual proportions, but one of the reasons people feel the need for detail is that it helps them find their way. Detail helps to fill up the empty holes on the canvas.

It is a common sight in an art class to see people hold up a pencil at the end of their outstretched arms. They are checking the size of one object against another. The pencil acts as a constant indication of size. It is not good to become dependent on this habit. A more rewarding method of comparing relative sizes is to look at the spaces between objects or around the figure you are drawing. If one observes and draws the shapes of these spaces accurately, they will give the essential clues to relative sizes. This is why the artist often draws the figure in a situation rather than isolated on a platform. Constant reference to related objects helps to form the space in which the figure stands.

Concentrating on drawing shapes between objects can lead to the type of composition seen in Art Nouveau in the late nineteenth century, Japanese prints, and the work of such artists as Lautrec, Beardsley and Bonnard. Here, figure-ground relationships are used to emphasize the surface pattern of the picture. Such pictures imply space more subtly than those using diagrammatic perspective.

It is important for the artist to grasp that space is never void. Once it is confronted as something that may be understood and utilized, it becomes a powerful force. It is inseparable from texture, rhythm, light, colour and line, for they are among the factors that define space.

Some rules

There are at least ten different ways of creating pictorial space that are constantly used. They are not all to be found in every painting, and some are ignored altogether by a few artists: **1** Two-dimensional or flat-pattern space, where depth is implied, not stated. This subtle approach may be seen in the work of those artists mentioned earlier in this chapter; **2** The overlapping of shapes which creates the illusion of three-dimensional space, one shape overlapping another appears as if it is in front of the other; **3** Linear perspective; **4** The relative size of shapes. Objects which, when placed next to each other in reality would be of equal size, appear to be separated by space when in a painting or drawing they are depicted as being of different sizes. The greater the

above left: **Kenneth Noland** (born 1924)
NIEUPORT acrylic on canvas 178 x 178 cm (70 x 70 in)

Colours interact with each other. This target appears to be continually enlarging and contracting, the small dot being overpowered by the large circle of blue. The large area of unpainted canvas gives the colour extra potency. The space these colours occupy appears undefined. See how the circle painted white has greater force than the dark red bulls eye, the splashes of blue swirling around the outside ring at first adds movement and on second viewing greater ambivalence. The varying space between the rings gives the colour independence.

above right: **Raoul Dufy** (1877–1953)
MADAME DUFY gouache 99.7 x 80.6 cm (39¼ x 31¾ in)

Dufy shows no inhibitions about using black paint for both lines and textures. He has nicely caught the posture of Madame sitting forward leaning on the table. The solid blue of the wall heightens the feeling of space and expectancy. Although the pattern of the tablecloth is relatively complicated, the portrait as a whole is simple, direct and has great decorative charm.

difference, the greater is the implied depth of space; **5** Focus. Objects in focus appear to be on a different plane to those out of focus; **6** Relative intensity of colour. Each colour relationship produces its own spatial effect; **7** The fact that cool colours tend to recede; **8** The contrast between values is less the further away they are from the spectator; **9** When considered separately, black recedes and white comes forward; **10** The experience felt of a particular space. Observation or a feeling for space is a means of creating pictorial space that does not rely on tricks or gimmicks, for it has to be understood during the process of painting. This 'emotive' space nevertheless uses some of the other nine factors.

'Emotive' space has much in common with 'atmospheric' space. It is difficult to describe, but once one has become involved in the activity of painting, one develops an awareness, if not a full understanding, of this type of spatial quality.

Viewing the masters

The work of two painters in particular is well worth looking at when you go to art galleries, for their mastery of atmospheric and emotively felt space. Both painters use the qualities of light as their major space-creating 'tool'. Turner is one, particularly in his later 'impressionistic' works, and Vermeer is the other. Because the quality is so subtle, it is necessary to describe the best way to look at Vermeer's work. First, look at it in the usual gallery-going way. Then sit comfortably in front of the painting, looking unhurriedly, but not staring, at it, letting yourself 'take it in'. You will soon become aware of how the space or air in the picture is tangible; you can feel the way it fills the room. If you practise this technique while looking at the pictures of Matisse, you will get a similarly heightened experience, but this time you will see subtle colour relationships not seen at the first glance.

Linear PERSPECTIVE

Linear perspective is a means of visually describing three-dimensional solids and their relationship to each other on a flat surface. There are other ways of drawing solids in space, some of which are described in the previous chapter. The artist needs to be aware that the laws of perspective are mechanical; they can be broken as often as seems sensible.

Linear perspective is generally understood to have been most fully developed during the Renaissance. Its more complete understanding was helped by the invention of the camera obscura—a large lightproof box into one wall of which was drilled a small hole. After sitting in the box for some time so that the eyes adjusted to the low level of light, a picture could be seen on the wall opposite the small hole. It was an upside-down version of the scene outside the box. This translation of the real world into a picture on a flat surface made it possible to understand the perspective of very complicated scenes.

The challenge

Perspective can be difficult to grasp for those who do not have both a visual and a mathematical mind. Even some nineteenth-century painters, such as Jean Millet and Edgar Degas, hired the help of a person who could advise them on perspective. Perspective can also be difficult to handle, for when its rules are too closely observed, the results look artificial and unconvincing.

A further complication arises when we consider that we look with two eyes, and the brain puts the two images together as one. This ability to see two angles of an object at once is compounded by the way we are able to move our heads from side to side. Some masters of the Renaissance used fixed-point perspective. In this system it was necessary to stand on a prescribed spot in front of the painting in order to get the full effect of three-dimensional realism.

Bearing in mind these complexities, the following is a short introduction to simple perspective: 1 Parallel perspective is a form of perspective used by artists of the Far East. The artist will show, for example, each side of a box square on to the viewer. It is possible with parallel perspective to see base, top, front and two sides all at the same time. As images move up the picture the viewer understands that he is seeing them move into the distance, instead of their being foreshortened, that is, growing smaller as they recede. Grandma Moses uses a similar method—see page 12. 2 Single or central-point perspective is a simple form of perspective used by Western painters. In this type of perspective all lines that are at right angles to the surface of the picture (the 'picture plane') would, if they were extended, or projected towards the back of the picture, meet at one point. This point ('vanishing point') is on a line called the horizon, which is at the same level as the painter's eye. 3 A third form of perspective is two-point (angular). Again, there is the conventional horizon. Instead of projected lines meeting at one vanishing point on the horizon, they meet at two points. The lines on the left of the solid meet on the left and the lines on the right meet at the right. The same two vanishing points are shared by all those objects that share the same angle to the picture plane. These angles can be mathematically worked out, but for most paintings this is not necessary if the solids are being drawn from observation rather than plans or the imagination. 4 The fourth form of perspective is three-point or triaxial perspective. This is normally only used when the object is well above or a long way below the eye level. Just as horizontal lines moving away from the eye go to the horizon, so vertical lines can go to points on a line that is above the top of the picture, or to a line well below. To which line, above or below, depends on the situation of the object in relation to the eye level. A number of technical illustrators, but very few painters, concern themselves with triaxial perspective. A simple way of seeing this form of perspective is to look in a convex mirror; the reflection is an exaggerated form of triaxial perspective. These three forms of perspective: central point, angular and triaxial can be used to great effect in the same work of art.

The key line and points

The most important point to remember in perspective is that all horizontal lines which are not parallel to the picture plane would, if projected, meet on the horizon, which is at the artist's eye level.

If the vertical sides of the object cross over the eye level, then unless the box is transparent, neither its top nor bottom surfaces are visible.

In the accompanying illustrations the side of the box has been divided into equal areas. It can be seen clearly that the eye sees more of the areas towards the front than of those at the back.

A circle has been drawn over the divided-up side of the box. It can be seen that it also changes shape as it becomes foreshortened and disappears from view. Note that the ends of the ellipse are round, not pointed.

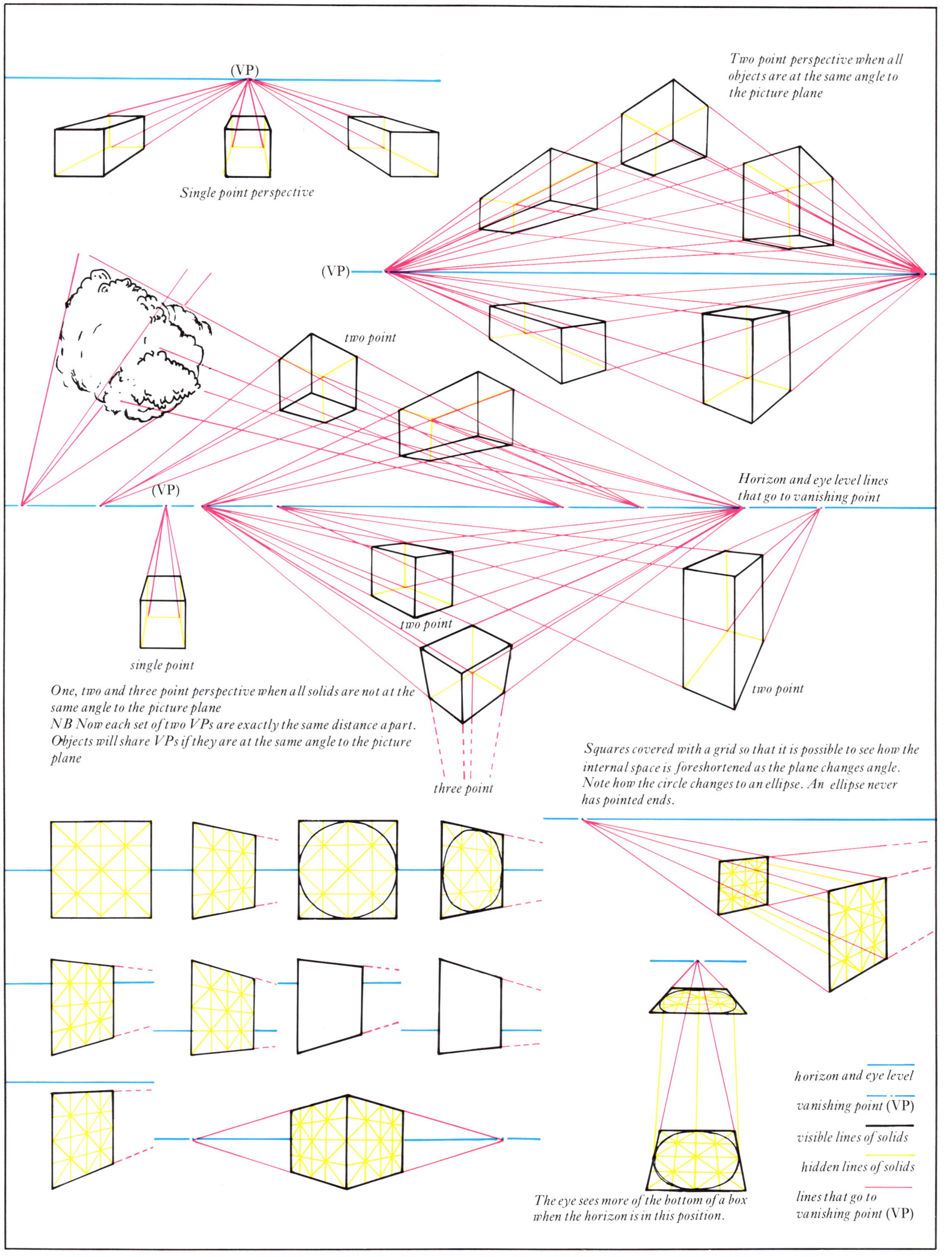
(VP)
Single point perspective
Two point perspective when all objects are at the same angle to the picture plane
(VP)
two point
(VP)
Horizon and eye level lines that go to vanishing point
two point
single point
two point
One, two and three point perspective when all solids are not at the same angle to the picture plane
NB Now each set of two VPs are exactly the same distance apart. Objects will share VPs if they are at the same angle to the picture plane
three point
Squares covered with a grid so that it is possible to see how the internal space is foreshortened as the plane changes angle. Note how the circle changes to an ellipse. An ellipse never has pointed ends.
horizon and eye level
vanishing point (VP)
visible lines of solids
hidden lines of solids
lines that go to vanishing point (VP)
The eye sees more of the bottom of a box when the horizon is in this position.

LINE, RHYTHM and TEXTURE

Children begin to explore their new world through their fingers, bodies and mouths. They discover and familiarize themselves with the textures and shapes they are allowed to touch and feel, thus developing their tactile sense and extending their experience. Sight is almost the last sense to be put to use, and then it is usually only for visual recognition for future reference.

The re-occurrence for a child of the visual appearance of a shape or texture stimulates a response which might be a feeling of warmth, hunger or disgust. After a while, the system is short-circuited by the child's being aware of similar textures and superimposing a memory from past experience of what they might feel like. Touching becomes inhibited and declines, while the child begins to rely on his memory of tactile quality.

Children hate trying out new foods, and make their decision on sight alone. Only with maturity is enough confidence gained to try out new foods for tactile sensations. Similarly, unless a drawing or painting is a pictorial representation of a recognizable subject, it takes courage and perseverance to acquire the taste for its enjoyment.

below: **Vincent van Gogh** (1853–1890)
THE HARVEST oil on canvas 72.5 x 92 cm ($28\frac{1}{2}$ x $36\frac{1}{4}$ in)

In spite of the horizontal lines made by the fences and boundaries of the fields, the eye is forced by the spikes to move upwards from the bottom of the picture. The peaceful area of the sky invites the eye to come down again, stopping perhaps at the horse and cart. In this painting the eye cannot rest, which might indicate the traumatic character of the artist.

Catching the beat

Even the most primitive societies develop sophisticated, rhythmic, musical systems. The painter's art is to capture the essence of rhythm. A drawing or painting without rhythm is as incomplete as a poem or a piece of music without it. Visual rhythm is an essential ingredient of art. It can take many forms; rhythm is to be found in colours, lines, shapes, textures and space. Popular music is not ashamed to accentuate rhythm in all its musical forms, and its popularity certainly arises from this very fact.

The rhythmic arrangement and placing of shapes, textures and tone makes a significant contribution to the success of any painting or drawing. Shapes and masses must be ordered and controlled. Each shape has its own particular quality which reacts with the other shapes and their collective background. Yet movement in painting is not the same as restlessness. Calm, balance and serenity are equally powerful effects.

The following exercise is to help you see the dynamics of rhythm, texture and pattern as they work together.

One form of sculpture and painting is the 'feely'. This can be any shape, but let us say you give it the form of a long strip of paper. It involves finding and making textures as well as shapes that can be felt and translated through touch: fur, sequins, pinheads, sandpaper, smooth plastic sheeting—these are just some of the examples of the possible materials that might be used for tactile effect. The idea is to arrange these so that when blindfolded the 'viewer' is able to 'read' the painting through touch. This involves texture, rhythm and shape, and space that flows in an ordered manner.

Texture

below: **James Huguet** (1415–1492)
SAINT GEORGE AND THE PRINCESS (detail)
oil on wooden panel 87 x 55 cm ($34\frac{1}{4}$ x $21\frac{3}{4}$ in)

A geometrically composed painting. The rigid line that cuts across the top of the painting is softened by the strength of the golden halo. The use of scratched texture on the armour is enhanced by the plain expanse of sky. The trees, although they look as if part of a stage set, in that they are stuck like poles into the ground, have a simple elegance and charm. The natural elements of the painting—heads, hands and landscape—are depicted with a feeling of intimacy. The armour and weaponry are seen as decorative enhancements, painted with skill but with little emotion.

COMPOSING the picture

The composition or design of any painting or drawing has a great influence on the viewer's ability to follow, and to stay looking at, the work in question. In both painting and drawing the process of composition is a crucial ingredient, making it possible to return again and again to a picture with renewed enjoyment.

This does not mean that all paintings should be pleasant to look at, for some disturb or offend us by the nature of their subject matter. Many elements contribute to the composition of any painting or drawing. These are rhythm, line, shape, texture, tone, colour, light, perspective, space and tonal values. Composition is the way these elements are combined into a rhythmic, harmonious or in some other way of satisfying the whole. The eye wanders over the surface of the picture and also follows the lines that lead into its depths. It then finds other lines to lead it back to the surface. The art of composition is to provide these means for the eye to travel, sometimes vigorously, sometimes sedately, and also to find points of rest. Having gathered together those elements that make up a work of art, the task now is to produce a drawing or painting that grasps the viewer's attention and can be understood once the rules for that particular piece of work are perceived.

below: *To construct a golden mean rectangle draw two identical squares next to each other. Project a diagonal line through two opposite corners of the rectangle made by the two squares. With the aid of a set square draw a line from point A which is at right angles to the diagonal. Where this line cuts the diagonal draw line BC. The larger area remaining is a golden mean rectangle: it always contains a square and another golden mean rectangle.*

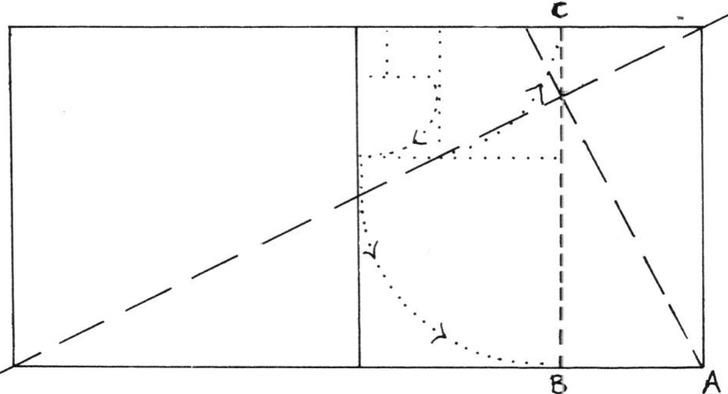

Deceiving the eye of the viewer

First and foremost, try to keep the work compositionally simple. Do not mix too many different approaches; use perspective *or* pattern. Some artists, place the stress or movement of their paintings on simple geometrical shapes such as a square, circle or triangle. Such shapes do not readily allow the eye to leave the canvas, and they bring order and unity into any work. Circles are harmonious and imply comfort. Oval shapes are associated with classical beauty and passiveness, but they lack strength and stamina; ovals are submissive. Horizontal lines imply calm, peace and balance. Vertical lines have more tension and suggest aspiration and uplift. Diagonal lines, however, introduce change, instability and movement. Their direction also indicates mood, and the speed of movement. In Western cultures, movement towards the right is flowing, while towards the left it indicates anxiety and force. A combination of diagonal, horizontal or vertical lines that makes a triangular shape can demonstrate dilemma as well as unity.

Being single-minded

During the early Renaissance, in the fourteenth century, artists rediscovered the possibilities of mathematical and geometric proportions as a means of composition. The most famous of all these seemingly magical formulas is the Golden Mean or Divine Proportion, which can be expressed as the ratio 1 to 1.618 (approximately 5:8). The claim is made that this proportion occurs frequently in Nature. Piero della Francesca gave up painting to concentrate on mathematics and wrote an important book on the subject. During the Renaissance, science, mathematics, geometry and art were closely linked, and painters were equally at ease manipulating numbers and pigments. After the seventeenth century painters lost this close familiarity with science and mathematics, and now find such systems of geometrical proportion difficult to handle; but geometry, whether used consciously or unconsciously, remains the basis of most compositional schemes.

A famous colourist, Wassily Kandinsky (1868–1944), outlined in his book *Concerning the Spiritual in Art* some helpful ways of considering the use of colour in composition. He believed that the eye reacted in different ways to different colours: 'If two circles are drawn and painted yellow and blue, a brief contemplation will reveal in the yellow spreading movement out from the centre, and a noticeable approach to the spectator. The blue, on the other hand, moves into itself, like a snail retreating into its shell. . . . The eye feels stung by the first circle (yellow) while absorbed into the second.'

Nature's own rules

Artists use light as one of their means of composition. It

top right: **Stanley Spencer** (1891–1959)
TRAVOYS ARRIVING WITH WOUNDED AT A DRESSING STATION AT SMOL IN MACEDONIA
oil on canvas 183 x 218.5 cm (72 x 86 in)

A deeply religious man, Spencer saw the war as a terrible drama. The structure of the linear composition with central point perspective of this 'stage set' is fairly self-evident. Like a photographer, the war artist has caught the moment for ever.

middle right: **Henri Matisse** (1869–1954)
THE DANCE oil on canvas 260 x 391 cm (102⅜ x 150⅝ in)
Powerful rhythms and co-ordinated movement are the essence of this mass of reds and blues. Every mark is elegant and economical. Matisse has avoided adding anything that detracts from the total effect. Each person is seen as an individual as well as part of the group. Matisse's sense of space is once again apparent as being simultaneously two- and three-dimensional.

below right: **Aubrey Beardsley** (1873–1898)
TRISTAN AND ISOLDE ink on paper
15.2 x 17.5 cm (5 x 6¾ in)

Beardsley was a master in handling the counterpoint of white spaces with black solids. His backgrounds do not form holes in the picture but act as positive pattern elements, used in this drawing sparingly and with great compositional effect. The eye leaps from the exposed bosoms to the hand in the top right-hand corner down to the figures' feet and across to the sash, finally to the hand resting on the dress. One side of the drawing is neatly balanced by the other.

is used as a means of directing the eyes, which are attracted by brightness and luminosity, towards a chosen area. As a relief from this brightness, the eyes are inclined to look into shadows and semi-darkness, then jump back into the bright luminous area. Middle tone areas will be seen, but not so consciously taken in as the extremes of light and dark. It is in these middle tone areas that the eye is not so conscious of absorbing information, a fact well known by designers of advertisements.

Nature, as is well known, seeks harmony and balance. Nature also abhors a vacuum, and will find every possible way to fill it. The difficulty is that the moment the eye has found peace and rest, it searches once more for movement, before flicking back to rest, and so on. It is desirable, therefore, to ensure that the eye is not led to search for either movement or rest outside the picture area. Texture and pattern need to be balanced against areas of comparative quietness. There is also a strong tendency for the Western eye to be pulled down into the bottom right-hand corner of any painting because of the way we read! Some device may be necessary to ensure it is encouraged to look elsewhere within the picture area.

Competition

Dynamic tension is an important element in composition. A single mark, if well placed on a sheet of paper, can visually capture the whole area. It will build around itself a 'force field' of influence. A second mark, however, will be in opposition to the first. It will have its own force field, which will retreat from or encroach upon the other mark. Further marks will also compete for space, and will need to be placed on the picture area with different degrees of intensity.

Believing what you see

Here is a useful exercise for understanding a little about the way the human eye sees space in composition. It is a difficult exercise, for it takes much self-discipline.

Sit about six inches away from an obviously three-dimensional object. With a drawing board firmly propped in front of you, fix the eyes on one small spot on that object. Focus your eyes on that selected point. Do not let your eyes wander from it. Draw only what you see, not as you think you ought, or what you know of the object. At the edge of your vision will be some large hazy areas, while as you move in towards your selected focus area, images will become clearer and clearer until in the centre the focus will become sharp. I repeat: draw what you see, not allowing your eye to check what you think might be there on the edge of your vision. This drawing will take about an hour. Rest your eyes frequently, but try not to give up focusing on the one spot each time. The final result will be a form of vortex or whirlwind of activity, concentrating at the point of focus.

Why it happens

You will understand from this exercise a great deal about how we see. In particular you will understand that what we call normal vision is a composite image made up of many such images with different focus points. The eye moves across, over, into and out of space, and the brain combines the separate images into one. This process seems to be both instantaneous and continuous.

There are no formulas or sure-fire ways of producing a well-composed picture. Design, organization, and composition give to any painting a sense of structure, a firm stability on which ideas can be built. The activity of painting and drawing is an equation between emotional response and defined direction. At the moment of painting the activity can so absorb our attention that we forget to think consciously. We rightly rely on our subconscious and let our enjoyment coupled with understanding and knowledge of what we are painting guide our sensibilities. A sound understanding of composition and design enables all works to have a visual strength that gives the viewer the feeling that the particular work he is looking at was painted by someone with firm ideas and creative ability.

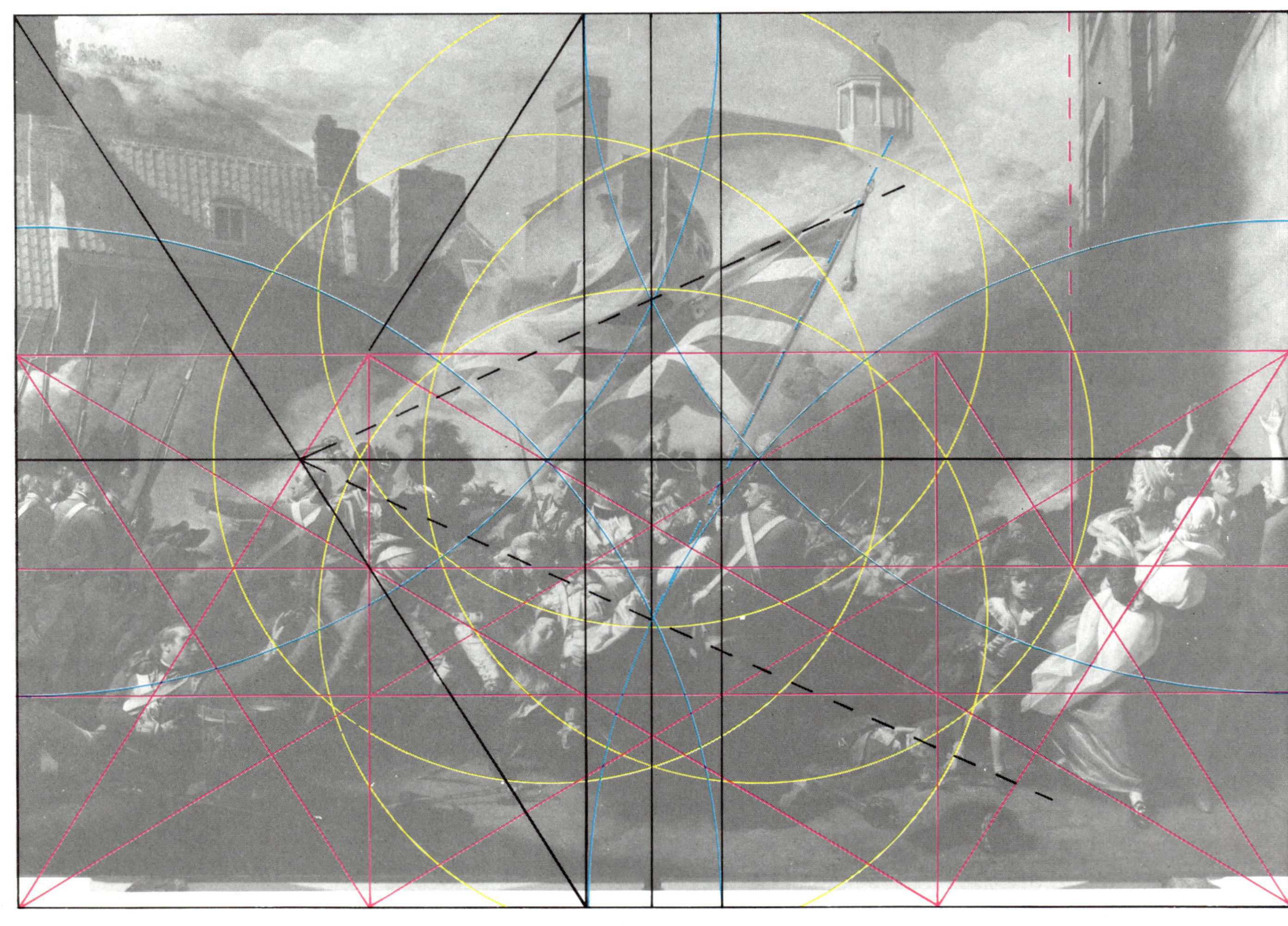

left: **Pierre Bonnard**
(1867–1947)
THE TABLE oil on canvas
103.8 x 74.3 cm ($40\frac{1}{2}$ x $29\frac{1}{4}$ in)

The artist has in this painting shown how he has felt his way across the table. He has lovingly painted each individual object. The cloth is painted as a mist that swirls around the base of each object. Linear perspective has been stretched and changed to suit the needs of the painter. Together these enhance the magical appearance of the whole scene. The figure to ground relationship has become inseparable. Bonnard's blues are strengthened and enhanced by touches of concentrated yellows—blue's contrasting colour. The composition of the work is basically simple. The edge of the table leads the eye from the bottom left-hand corner around the canvas to the girl helping herself to food. The curve of her shoulder brings the eye back to the table down to the large restful area of white in the bottom right-hand corner. Within the painting there are rhythms that are less obvious but just as powerful—for example, the diagonal layout of the objects on the table, which gives the viewer a sense of unease.

opposite: For details of this painting by **Copley**, see page 41

To analyse the composition of this or any other painting, one must first look for clues in the lines of objects, buildings, gestures etc. and continue these lines to the edge of the picture. Where these intersect each other or the frame, horizontal or vertical lines are drawn to find which ones are the key constructional lines. This analysis showed that there is a narrow strip missing at the bottom of this picture, as many of the significant lines converge on a line outside the frame. Overlapping 'golden mean' systems are used in this picture. These are positioned in relation to the two squares formed by drawing arcs from the four corners. The basic lines of one of the golden mean systems are shown in red. If you make a tracing of this analysis and reposition it both upside-down and reversed you will see how the geometry is repeated in all quarters of the painting. Shown are some of the compositional lines made when key points are linked. Take a transparent ruler and discover for yourself how other lines follow through and relate to each other.

DRAWING and exploring

Drawing is the term used by artists for the activity of making and arranging marks. These marks can be made with any materials that make an image. Some of the media most frequently associated with drawing are lead pencils, charcoal and ink. The camera is favoured by many today, though it is a poor substitute for any of the conventional media.

Drawings, whatever way they are made, fall into one of the following categories: explanatory, doodle, emotional or responsive. Explanatory drawings are used as a means of exploring a particular aspect of the subject: for example, a drawing made in a sketchbook by a painter as a preliminary study. Doodles are the result of 'taking a line for a walk' on a surface; sometimes it is difficult, as has often been pointed out, to know when a line has stopped being a line and has turned into a shape. Or the line might explore arabesque patterns, or simply be a group of marks that combined to make little more than a pleasing image. The responsive drawing is one that flows from the inner emotions in response to what is seen or felt by the artist at that time. This can be made without analytical investigation, but always shows a definite and positive display of energy and confrontation. Most drawings contain an element of all these three categories.

Drawing pictures

Such forms of drawings include mechanical drawings, the scribbles of the very young, and the extravagant decorations of sculptured edifices such as Tutankhamun's tomb, as well as the dull products of those art students who do no more than fill a sheet of cartridge paper with pencil marks. An essential element in all good drawing, no matter what medium is used, is the desire of the artist to go beyond mere mark-making.

Communicating through drawing

Communication is an important objective of drawing. The police, for example, use a system of drawing known as Identikit in which the portrait of an individual is built up from a bank of pictures of facial features. Separate images combined together make an image of a face; the drawing has been made by an Identikit.

Handwriting is a pure form of communicative drawing. This may seem like stretching the definition too far, yet in placing words on a page we use our sense of space, texture and tone as well as rhythm, the memory of shapes and the ability to put things in order. The effectiveness and quality of the communication depends on the same criteria as are used in making any other kind of drawing.

Referring to handwriting as a form of drawing might be considered a digression from purposeful discussion of what is usually understood to be drawing: the marks that depict landscape, figure and still life. My purpose in referring to non-figurative drawing is to demonstrate that the process of drawing is not limited to the making of pictorial images but can be seen as underlying a much wider range of making and doing activities.

Keep it simple

Anything can be the subject of a drawing. There is nothing too insignificant to draw. A note of caution, however, should you be tempted to tackle a complicated subject: in order to satisfy yourself you may find yourself spending a long time and the process may well become over-demanding and frustrating. Allow yourself some experience of visual filtering and selecting before trying to draw a complex subject.

When beginning the process of discovery through drawing, the medium you use is often your most useful aid. The feel of a soft pencil, and the sort of marks and images it forms, can be as exciting as the subject you are investigating. I suggest you start with a very soft pencil, such as a 4B, or a steel pen and ink.

Choose a subject with which you are conversant. If you are a gardener, why not draw a plant, tools, or a corner of the potting shed or greenhouse? Remember at this stage the intention is not to produce a work of art that is to be framed. The purpose of the exercise is to introduce you to the idea of discovering new images through drawing.

Using a viewfinder

Cover the whole surface of your paper with dots or marks of varying sizes, say, 40 marks in all, without looking at the subject. Make an adjustable frame or viewfinder from two L-shaped pieces of card. Looking through this frame, you will see that some parts of the framed area are more prominent than others, perhaps because they are darker or lighter, or in some other way attract your attention. Some of the marks you have made will already be in the 'right' place for your drawing. The marks also serve to destroy the whiteness and cleanliness of the paper, which might inhibit your studies. Make sure your rubber eraser is well out of reach, preferably in another room, and begin purposefully to draw in the spaces

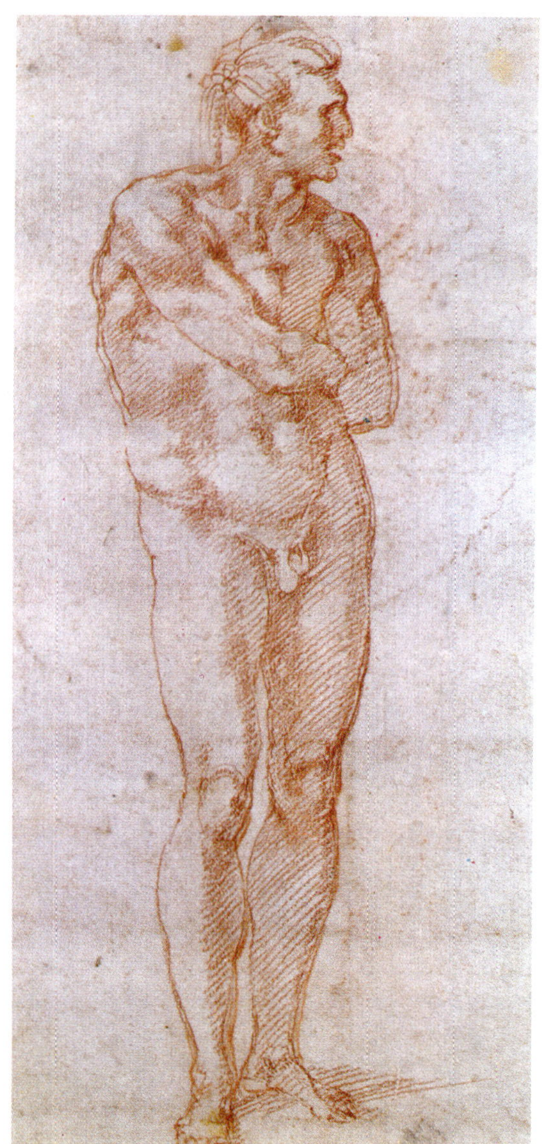

left: **Michelangelo Buonarotti** (1475–1564)
MALE NUDE red chalk 28.9 x 18.1 cm ($11\frac{3}{8}$ x $7\frac{1}{8}$ in)

A subtle drawing that shows the artist has considerable anatomical knowledge. The drawn line is sensitive rather than tentative. The torso is shown as foreshortened as the drawing moves around to the back. The figure is standing firmly with the weight beautifully distributed throughout the body.

below: **Alexander Cozens** (1717–1786)
WEYMOUTH HARBOUR WITH PORTLAND IN THE DISTANCE pen and watercolour 20.6 x 27.9 cm ($8\frac{1}{8}$ x 11 in)

Both observed and invented, this drawing describes quite clearly some of the qualities of the landscape. The trees appear as bubbles interrupting the smoothly eroded hills. The clouds, as a contrast, are jagged, casting their shadows across the foreground, leading one's eye down to the harbour.

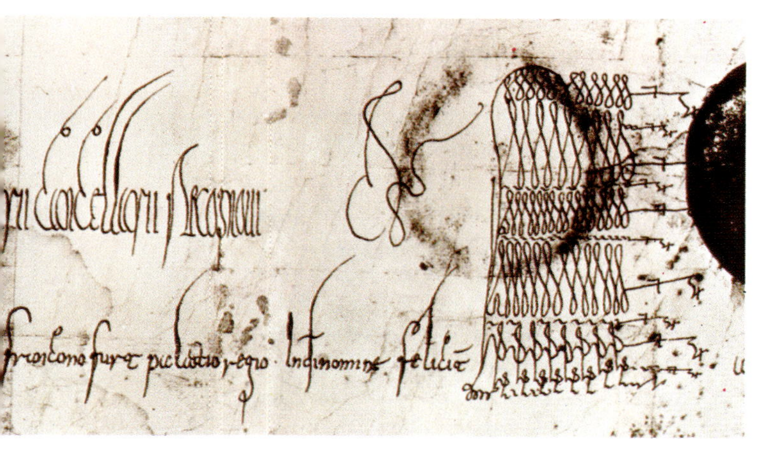

above left: **Chancellor Walto,** around 859
SIGNATURE

Great style and free-flowing elegance in this rhythmical line is used as the visual identity of this pedantic artist.

above right: **Church of the Transfiguration,** Kizhi, 1714
WOODEN ROOFS photograph
These wooden blocks were drawn, that is, cut out with a saw. Their purpose is to look good as well as to function well technically. The photograph acts as a drawing in that it is a record in line, tone and colour.

around, inside and outside the objects and background shapes, starting with the prominent parts and working backwards or forwards in space. Do not lift your pencil off the paper until the drawing is finished but keep working backwards and forwards in the space of the picture. Vary the intensity of your line according to the needs of the composition. Draw as quickly as possible, looking much more often at your subject than the paper. Do not let an inability to draw straight lines stop you working. This drawing is not to be an accurate representation of reality but a collection of shapes locking together. As you proceed, dodging from one area to another without lifting your pencil, the sheet will become blacker and blacker. Do not worry if your drawing looks 'messy'. 'Tidiness', said Vernon Blake in 1929, 'covers a multitude of artistic sins. An exponent of it hardly looks at the model (subject) at all while drawing. His only preoccupation is drawing. He should give an undivided attention to the study of the model. . . . Never work as a dry-as-dust grammarian. But always, even when studying, work as a poet.'

Stand well back

One of the most successful ways of drawing is to stand at the drawing board, which is firmly positioned on an easel. Try holding your drawing implement slightly less than an arm's length away from the board, so that it will touch the paper fairly easily. At first your arm may shake, so with your free arm, prop up your drawing elbow. In this position you can see both drawing and subject and by standing well back from the drawing you can see it as a whole. Use your whole arm when drawing to make sweeping strokes. Stand on your toes so that your body feels alert and free and let your whole body move in response to the rhythms of the drawing. It is as if you were 'dancing' the drawing, the pen or pencils being an extension of your arm and body. Many professional artists, by the way, find that their work becomes cramped and uneasy when they fall into the trap of using their pencil or brush as they would a writing implement.

Using the whole of the paper is important. You do not have to cover every square inch with lines or textures; make use of space, remembering that no object or figure stands in isolation. The space around objects, as I said in the chapter on feeling for space (page 22), gives them solidity and depth. Balance the subject in the picture area. Leonardo's and Michelangelo's sketches were always so well placed on the page that each sheet makes a satisfying composition.

It is not always necessary to draw a continuous line around objects. Where the tone of the object is the same as that of the background, there is no visible difference to mark. Matisse, for instance, draws in the background with the same intensity as the figure. The subject for him is the total environment including the model. This approach gives the work an ambivalence between shapes and forms.

Pictures in the mind's eye

You may find, when you have completed a number of drawings, that the results are not as exciting as you had imagined or hoped they would be. This is probably because you had a preconceived idea about the finished picture. If you try to reproduce preconceived ideas on paper, you will not allow your ideas to grow or change. Any rigidity or preconception can too easily stop you developing a sense of discovery. You may also have felt frustrated that you were advised not to use an eraser. However, the purpose of drawing is not learning how to correct; rather, it is about making decisions.

We have all seen pictures in the fire, in cloud shapes, or in stains on walls. Alexander Cozens, the eighteenth-century landscape painter, developed a unique way of using this imaginative ability. With a sable brush and black ink he made little marks or blots very close together on a sheet of white paper. Then, relaxing and half-closing his eyes, he let the imagination roam over the marks. Try to do this. Your mind will make objects or familiar shapes out of the marks. You will soon see how with a little effort it is possible to build up and develop these images. Do this quickly, then look at the new blot picture. This in turn will stimulate your imagination to another version. After about half an hour you will have

left: *BAYEUX TAPESTRY*
(about 1077) wool on cloth
height 50 cm ($19\frac{1}{2}$ in)

A fine drawing, made by embroidering with eight different coloured wools. The artist working on this section wanted to describe the emotions of the people involved; notice the animation in their hands and how well they are drawn. Each man has a personality of his own, unlike the icon paintings that were being made in Central Europe at the same time.

opposite: **David Clark**
(born 1963)
NUDE IN MOVEMENT
powder colour on newsprint
74.6 x 45.7 cm (30 x 18 in)

This drawing took less than a minute to make; it was the twentieth in a series of forty executed within an hour, each one building on the knowledge gained from the ones before.

produced a drawing or composition entirely from your imagination and the images you have mentally stored away in the past.

Stretching the mind

Tony Buzan, in his BBC radio broadcasts about imagination and memory, talks of the usefulness of trying to recall at the end of the day everything that has occurred to you. By taking the time to remember each incident as it happened, the mind is refreshed and the memory strengthened. The artist, however, can go one stage further. Try to sketch from memory faces and incidents that occurred during the day.

Most drawing instructors discourage copying, saying that it is better for people to produce their own work, and not acquire second-hand knowledge. But why not be your own favourite draughtsman for a while, instead of copying him? This is an exercise in pastiche. A pastiche is a work in the manner of someone else, or in a particular style. It is very different from being a careful copy. Theatre designers, for example, use pastiche to distil the flavour of a past period.

Make an expedition to your local library and choose a book on a draughtsman whose work inspires or attracts you. Look at a drawing that you admire of this artist and try to put yourself in his shoes, so that you understand why he chose that particular subject, and why he drew as he did, and also his reasons for using certain materials and equipment. Now choose a subject you think might have attracted your master draughtsman and, if possible with the same materials, make a drawing in his manner. This may well mean looking a little into his history and background. In this way you will gain unexpected insights both into the artist and into the nature of drawing.

Keep them vital

It is essential to keep your work fresh. A drawing session can extend over several days, but at first you should not tackle subjects that need so much time. If while you are working on it a drawing feels as if it is taking too long, it will probably look laboured and tired. One way of keeping work vital is to use an unfamiliar medium. Exploit your chosen media to the full, but do not be afraid of trying out new ones.

Find some small black and white objects and place them on a sheet of white paper, lit with lighting as dramatic as possible. With a small artist's sponge, and some liquid black paint mixed to the consistency of milk, rough in a wash on your drawing paper so as to divide the work into black and white areas. Remember to compose the picture area. Do not worry that the sponge

makes crude marks. Crude or less sophisticated statements are often very compelling if they are made with conviction, rather than laziness. Work close to the subject and involve the background, too. Hold your sponge at arm's length, gradually making the tone darker and darker, but without going into detail. Keep the masses broad and large. Do not forget that it is more important to look at the subject than the drawing. After a few moments, stop and assess the balance you have made in tone between the black and the white. Whites are hardly ever seen in nature, and they could well appear in your work to be holes bored through the paper. I

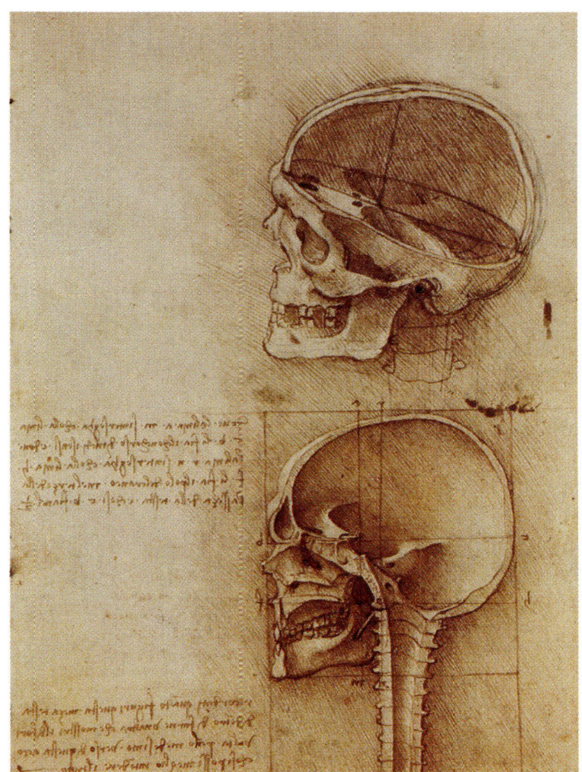

suggest you leave no white areas at all. The object of this drawing is to explore the effects of light without the complications of colour.

Having another go

When you have done as much as you can with your first drawing, take a clean sheet of paper and start again. Ask yourself what you have learned and what questions you have left unanswered. Try to show how you see the effects of light rather than trying to reproduce exactly what you see. The second drawing will reinforce what you learned from the first, and also help you to see the subject afresh. Resist the temptation to copy the first drawing. One excellent draughtswoman says that each time she begins a piece of work she thinks that it will be easier to execute than the last. It never is. Every time, she says, she has to ask herself questions more fundamental than ever before.

Tone is not colour

Colour in drawing often presents difficulties to the beginner. There is no reason why it should, once one realizes that one is dealing with tone, not colour. If the subject is a dark-coloured object in shadow, there may be no need to draw the object in a darker tone than its shadow. Treat the colours as tones, and try to keep them consistent in each drawing. You may decide in a particular instance, for good reasons, to treat bright colours as dark tones. If you must be inconsistent, however, remember that rules should only be broken or altered for a purpose.

There is sometimes confusion, when working with pencil, pen or charcoal, about the direction of tonal

right: **Sharaku**
(about 1794)
THE ACTOR MORITA KANYA VIII
woodcut on Japanese paper
37.3 x 24.8 cm ($14\frac{3}{4}$ x $9\frac{3}{4}$ in)

Woodcut, like all forms of print-making, is an excellent discipline for the draughtsman. Print-making is a form of true artistry, for it combines physical skills with visual sensibilities. The drawing process is one of reverse, that is, each line printed is the remains of a surface that has been cut away. Some multi-colour prints were produced by putting together as a jigsaw the pre-inked segments, then taking the print. In this drawing the bold shapes express the forceful nature of the actor's character.

opposite: **Leonardo da Vinci**
(1452–1519)
TWO SECTIONS OF THE SKULL
pen and ink on faded white paper
27.9 x 20 cm (11 x $7\frac{7}{8}$ in)

Mathematics and its relationship to natural forms is a major part of the investigation made in these two drawings. Nothing was too much trouble; the skull was first cut open one way, and then another. Each time different information was extracted, examined and recorded.

marks. This depends on the purpose of the drawing. In a preliminary drawing for a piece of sculpture, for example, it might be as well to follow the form, the drawing's purpose being to describe as closely as possible the subtleties of the shape of the intended sculpture. Ultimately, however, the right mark is the one that does the task required: demonstrating the process of searching.

Lino-cutting is drawing

One practical and exciting way of drawing is by lino-cutting. Most good art shops stock lino already cut to different sizes, together with the tools you will need, rollers, water-soluble ink and a simple instruction book. Sketch out your drawing onto the lino with white paint. Work in reverse, cutting away the areas you do not want to print. To take a print clean lino surface. Roll out a film of ink on a sheet of glass and then on to lino. Lay a piece of thin soft paper on to the inked surface and rub it gently and firmly with the bowl of a large spoon. Peel away the paper and inspect the print. Continue cutting the lino and taking prints until you are satisfied with the results. Keep the trial prints for reference on how the print developed.

For your first lino-cuts try cutting varied textures in adjacent squares. Make each texture as different as you can from the one next to it. Later use some of these textures you have invented in a pictorial lino-cut.

OILS

Legend has it that oil painting was invented by the Flemish painter Hubert van Eyck (1366?–1426). It was probably much more of a gradual development. Protective oils and varnishes would have been developed for practical purposes in the damp, rainy Netherlands sooner than in sunny Italy. When they were applied to picture-making their versatility attracted the interest of the Renaissance masters.

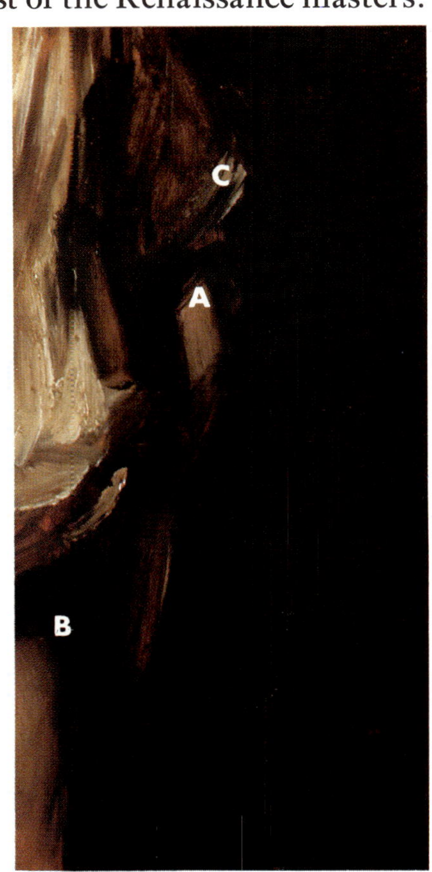

Oil paints are versatile because they can be used as thin transparent glazes of colour over solid under-painting, even over tempera paintings, or for solid opaque painting. It can be easy-flowing and achieve the smoothness and gloss of glass; or it can be applied in rich, thick paint, retaining the marks of the brush's movement in the technique known as impasto. A disadvantage of the medium is that it requires some technical knowledge to produce paintings that will not crack, fade or deteriorate, and to get maximum effect out of the medium.

The range of possible techniques is large: glazes over glazes; impasto by brush or palette knife; dabbing opaque colours over coloured grounds or under-paintings without obliterating them ('scumbling'); painting 'wet in wet' as when an opaque colour is applied to a tacky varnish coating.

above: **Rembrandt van Rijn,** *A WOMAN BATHING IN A STREAM* (detail)
A *brown wash underpainting with a bold impasto white brush stroke defining edge;* **B** *bold impasto drawing over underpainting, cool tones are produced by the 'turbid medium' effect;* **C** *the highlight area is produced by a lightly-dragged or stroked brush*

top left: **J. M. W. Turner,** *ULYSSES DERIDING POLYPHEMUS* (detail)
A *the whites lightly-painted into wet glazes;* **B** *scumbling: the loaded brush dragged lightly over an area glossed with pinks and purples;* **C** *the whites and near-whites spread with a painting knife;* **D** *bold impasto modified with delicate warm glazes*

centre left: **Edouard Vuillard,** *THE MANTELPIECE* (detail)
Alla prima approach loosely painted with well-diluted colours.

The medium of oil dries slowly and attempts to hasten the process or apply second coatings too soon can make the painting muddy or impermanent. Nevertheless, it rewards the effort of learning about its technicalities with, probably, the most sensuous handling medium ever invented.

The parts of an oil painting: 1 The support of wood panels, hardboard, stretched linen or cotton fabric, etc.; 2 The priming or sizing coat which isolates and protects the ground, and evens out the absorbency; 3 The ground which provides a satisfactory surface on which to paint; 4 The underpainting which should be diluted and contain less oil than subsequent coats—in some techniques it can be allowed to show through in parts having received glazes or scumbles over it; 5 The upper layers of the painting proper, which can consist of glazes, scumbles, impastos, areas of smooth opaque paint, or any mix of these; 6 A protective layer of retouching varnish—varnish can also be used between coats of paint. Each of the layers of the painting must be touch-dry before the next is applied.

The pigments for oil painting consist of minerals and organic materials, some modern chemical pigments and natural earth or crushed rocks. Some pigments are naturally transparent and some opaque. Some colours are not very permanent and should be avoided no matter how delicious they might seem.

Binding media

The colours are ground in an oil that hardens on exposure to air. The best known-drying oils are linseed and poppy. Poppy oil is used for some colours as it yellows less than linseed oil. White lead has been used as the main white for artists' oil paint for centuries, as it reacts chemically with linseed oil to produce a very strong flexible film (lead linoleate). Some artists for this reason recommend using a touch of white lead even in transparent glazes. Zinc white stays whiter but produces a more brittle film.

Resins, which are the gums from certain trees, are used both as protective varnishes and for mixing with the oil paint to give different handling qualities. Beeswax can also be used as a varnish or additive and can give a nice buttery feel to the paint. It is complicated to prepare and is best bought readymade from the colourman.

Thinning media consist mainly of turpentine and turps substitute or white spirit. Cheap turpentine turns brown and sticky in time; double-distilled genuine gum turpentine is expensive but necessary. White spirit is cheap, innocent of faults, but has no 'quality'. It is best used for primings, undercoats and sketches.

Glues and sizes can be had in very refined forms, from rabbit skin to parchment clippings, or in less expensive forms such as Scotch glue or concentrated glue size.

Standing v. sitting

The basic tools needed are palette, brushes, dippers, palette knife and lots of good, clean rags. The traditional wooden thumbhole palette is still preferred by many, not just because it looks romantically 'arty' but because

Stretching canvas

The canvas is 4 in larger all round than the stretcher frame. Canvas tacks are better than carpet tacks.

Squaring up the frame with a set square. NB The outside edge of frame is thicker than the inner.

From the middle, pin canvas with a tack. So it can be removed easily, do not drive home.

Turn and with grips pull canvas tight across frame. Now work north, south, east and west.

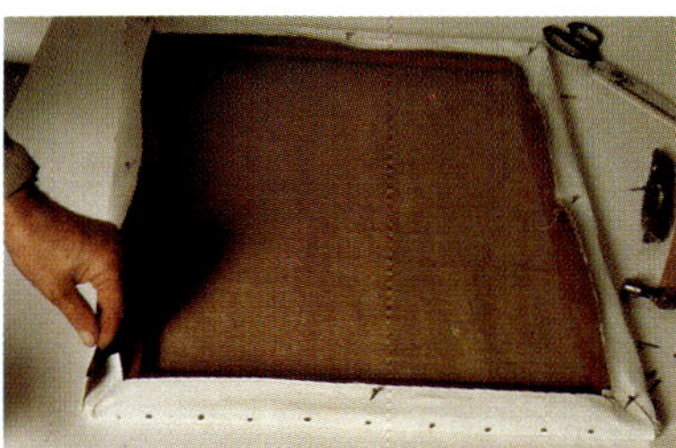

When canvas is tacked all round, and its grain is straight, drive home tacks, which are about 2 in apart.

Trim canvas back, having tacked it down. Drive in wedges to give stretcher an extra firm shape.

above: **James McNeill Whistler** (1837–1903)
AT THE PIANO oil on canvas 66 x 90 cm (26 x 35½ in)

The solid dark shapes of the piano, as well as the mother and her clothes, are interrupted by the light colours of the girl's dress. Painted in a bold manner it acts as a contrast to the smooth reflections in the picture glass. The two separate frames provide a gentle compositional link between the two dreaming faces of the mother and her daughter.

one can move around freely. Few painters sit down to paint. There are several reasons for this. Firstly, it is difficult for the artist to step back and look at the work as a whole. Most of us, when sitting, need considerable encouragement to get up on to our feet. Secondly, only half of the body is used if one sits; it is a good idea always to be on one's toes. Thirdly, sitting in a warm room, especially in a life room that needs to be heated to keep the model comfortable, tends to make people sleepy. Finally, it is sometimes useful to take a closer look at the subject matter, which many are reluctant to do if it means getting up!

The traditional brown wooden palette is appropriate for the traditional technique using a brown underpainting. When painting direct on to the white canvas it is better to lacquer the palette white. It is easier to see tonal and colour values when mixed on a surface similar to that of the canvas.

Large palettes are essential

A slab of glass on a table or serving trolley is the other main form of palette. The glass palette is easily scraped clean and can be submerged in water to prevent paint drying out. Generally the larger the palette the better. If the palette is not large enough the colours on it merge and the artist spends more time mixing fresh supplies of paint than looking at the subject. The larger the painting the larger the palette required. Some paintings contain large areas of flat colour. These can usually be mixed better in containers than on a flat surface. Some artists mix all their paint in cans and use these mixtures directly on the canvas.

Thumbhole palettes must be well balanced and comfortable to hold. A home-made plywood version copied exactly from the real thing can be balanced with a lead weight fixed underneath. You will need to experiment with handling the palette to find out where to place the weight. Sand the thumbhole to a comfortable finish.

Containers for oil and turpentine should be of reasonable size; a jam jar half full of white spirit is useful for cleaning brushes while painting. The containers that clip on to the edge of the palette are called dippers.

The painter in oils can hardly ever have enough brushes; a variety of shapes and sizes is desirable to create different effects and also to keep colours clean and separate. The one-brush painter is constantly having to

left:
John Singleton Copley
(1788–1815)
THE DEATH OF MAJOR PIERSON
oil on canvas
251.5 x 365.8 cm (99 x 144 in)

This large painting is packed with information and detail, all necessary for this is a visual record of a great event. Major Pierson died in 1781 is St. Helier, Jersey fighting the French. The artist makes fine and subtle use of the soft qualities of oils, to describe the effect of light meeting smoke.
See page 30 for a compositional analysis that shows how a painting may be examined for its underlying structure.

below: **Some surfaces to paint upon**

Top left to right: unprimed canvas, wooden door panel and plywood.
Bottom left to right: cardboard, brown craft paper, quality papers, hardboard with differing degrees of gesso. Underneath is ready primed canvas in a roll, together with tools and equipment needed for stretching a canvas.

stop and clean a brush or risk contaminating a white or delicate colour.

Good brushes are expensive, but cheap ones are a false economy. Brushes have a great effect on the 'hand-writing' of a painting. Cheap, stubby, shapeless brushes hinder rather than help, and can quickly discourage the beginner. A good round, long-bristled hog brush gives a greater variety of touch than one that is thin and flat. Flat brushes should not be too thin, and a 'filbert' shape is the most satisfactory. Sable-hair oil brushes are delightful tools.

Loving care

Do not buy cheap brushes, but care lovingly for the ones you have. Rinse the paint out in solvent. Using tepid water, rub the brush gently on to a bar of hard soap to produce a lather and work the brush into the palm of the hand to ease out the paint. Rinse thoroughly in warm water and suck or draw the bristles into shape. Keep the handles and metal ferrules clean too.

Easels or supports for holding the canvas come in a variety of shapes and sizes. All of them cost a lot of money. However, they are probably necessary. The first requirement of an easel is that it should hold the canvas firmly and be able to stand squarely on its feet. Some easels are designed to bend in the middle, so that it is possible to sit at them. Others have extra holding devices for securing the sketchpad.

Most easels are clumsy, inclined to fall over, and rarely hold the canvas properly without force. They are often delivered in a box to be made up. Make sure yours is stable before you pay for it. Some artists work without easels. One way is to lay the work surface flat on the floor and paint standing over it, feet either side. Unfortunately it is difficult to apply oil- or acrylic-bound media without a suitable means of supporting the surface.

The ideal and most responsive support for oil painting is canvas. Linen canvas is more stable than cotton. It can be bought ready primed. Unprimed, raw canvas can be bought by mail order from a merchant such as Russell and Chappell Ltd, 23 Monmouth Street, London WC2H 9DE (tel. 01-836 7521).

The canvas is stretched tautly and evenly over a wooden frame or stretcher and secured by canvas tacks. Wedges in each corner are used gently to tighten the canvas after it has been primed and sized. Hardboard or masonite is very widely used as a permanent support. The smooth side is best, but needs to be lightly sanded to break down the 'skin'.

Stretched paper can also be used for oil painting; see chapter on Watercolours (page 46).

The support whatever it is must first be sealed with a thin coat or two of glue size. Follow the instructions on the packet. Too strong a solution or too thick a coating is liable to crack. On hardboard the next coat can be a mixture of glue size and chalk. On canvas it should be a more flexible layer, traditionally a white lead in oil undercoat. White lead is poisonous and needs careful storage and use. Two coats are usually necessary and an oil ground should ideally have six months' drying-out time before use.

On hardboard two coats of acrylic primer without the layer of glue size makes a very good and reliable surface for painters today. Acrylic primer dries hard within the hour and is a valuable addition to the range of artists' materials available. Household emulsion paints are not recommended. It is possible that acrylic primers will prove equally satisfactory on non-rigid supports such as canvas, but this has not yet been proved by the test of time.

The painting itself

A number of ready-prepared, canvas-textured boards are available, such as Dalerboards, and these are relatively inexpensive.

So—how to start the real business of painting? First you must choose a range or 'palette' of colours appropriate to the subject or your intentions. The following is useful and adequate for a first palette: flake white, yellow ochre, Venetian red (warm), Indian red (cool), opaque oxide of chromium (green), cobalt blue, charcoal grey. These are mostly earth colours. An eight-colour palette could consist of flake white, raw umber, cadmium yellow, Venetian red, crimson alizarine, ultramarine, cobalt blue and viridian.

Add colours gradually to a basic palette and experiment with their use. Try substituting one colour for another to see what happens, e.g. cerulean for cobalt blue, or light red for Venetian red. You will soon know your way around the range of permanent colours.

above: **J. M. W. Turner** (1775–1857)
SNOW STORM oil on canvas 91.5 x 122 cm (36 x 48 in)

In the interests of technical accuracy, so that this painting should reflect the real nature of light, the artist was lashed to the mast of a ship during a snow storm. It was important to him to experience what he was describing. Turner was extremely shortsighted and refused when painting to wear glasses. This would account in part for his way of applying pigment in a swirling and revolving movement.

Fat over lean

Start your painting in a free fluid manner with well-diluted paint. Blocking in the masses in brown or grey will provide a good basis, when dry, for subsequent layers. These can be glazes, scumbles or impasto. Never use more medium than necessary. Always paint 'fat over lean', that is, let each layer contain more oil than the one beneath it. If parts of the painting go flat or dead on drying use retouching varnish to restore them before over-painting.

As binding liquids, or media, all you need are two simple ingredients of good quality: linseed oil and turpentine. Avoid a mess of half-understood complicated recipes. On the other hand, do not be afraid to experiment occasionally in order to extend your range.

Everything said so far in this chapter seems to have been about techniques. Because oil is a technically sophisticated medium it has led to expression and technique becoming intimately linked. You can therefore derive pleasure from a painter's work on the level of its majesty or its intimacy, its charm or its pathos and at the same time enjoy the handling of the paint, the 'handwriting', the tactile qualities of surface texture and the depths of coloured glazes. Once you have used the medium you will look at the paintings in galleries and museums with new understanding. You will see how the handling of the paint in, say, Leonardo, Rembrandt and

OILS

Rembrandt van Rijn
(1606–1669)
A WOMAN BATHING IN A STREAM oil on canvas
61.8 x 47 cm ($24\frac{1}{4}$ x $18\frac{1}{2}$ in)

Rembrandt wants us to feel with him his wife's pleasure in stepping through the water of a stream. He is able to convey this tender concern through very direct and forceful handling of the media. The rich reds and golds of the draperies, like those to be found in his larger, more elaborate paintings, are here achieved by very direct use of warm glazes and scumbled highlights. They contrast with the simplicity of the impastoed whited of the girl's slip, painted directly and vigorously over the brown wash underpainting. The 'turbid medium' effect comes into play here creating blue shadows in the shift. This painting seems to sum up a lifetime's technical know-how in a tiny, tenderly observed but vigorously handled painting.

Monet is quite different, yet totally appropriate to what they were trying to express.

Observing the masters

Observe the dragged or scumbled qualities of paint in a Chardin, how well it conveys the texture of freshly baked bread; see how the feel of a scrubbed pine table is conveyed, how appropriate the handling is to the intimate domestic interiors portrayed.

Look at the late works of Turner and observe how in paint he has managed to convey the impression of searing, disintegrating light. Compare these Turners with Monet's painting of light as something radiant, airy, springlike and see how different Monet's technique is and how it suits the message.

Look beneath the surface appearance to observe how the painting was built up. You will see that Courbet often paints over a coloured ground with a broken texture applied by knife or brush. Rubens has applied a broken wash of colour with brush or sponge over a brilliant white ground. Rembrandt's under-painting is similar, except that it is in the form of a preliminary drawing or 'grisaille' (meaning the areas of light and dark).

See how Van Gogh has taken the broken touches of colour of the Impressionists' techniques and allied them to the vigorous 'calligraphic' handling of Rembrandt to convey his own passionate intensity.

One could go on and on, but you must write the rest of these comparisons for yourself.

ACRYLICS

In the last sixty years there have been great advances in painting media. One of these is the development of an acrylic medium that can be painted onto any surface, including in some instances oil-bound ones. The colours are clear, bright and permanent, and while in their plastic state are soluble in water. Once set, acrylics are resistant to water, oil and changes in climate.

above left: **Mali Morris** (born 1945) *DOPSIC* (detail)

Some of the remarkable lively textures and colours that can be achieved through dry brush work and solid areas of pigment.

above: **Michael Moon** (born 1937) *OMEGA* (see page 73)

The texture of thinly applied pigments depends on the underlying surface. While the colours are not brilliant they are powerful.

Acrylics were developed in response to the needs of architects who wished to apply colour to the exteriors of buildings and to car manufacturers in search of surfaces resistant to wear. Both were also looking for a medium that would not change under hot and humid conditions.

These plastic media dry as quickly as water evaporates. They dry evenly through their porous surfaces and once dry do not dissolve in water. Because of this, extra care must be taken with brushes. The paint sets hard in the bristles, especially at the butt where they are bound by the metal ferrule. It then becomes impossible to make the bristles come together again to a point. Special brushes for use with acrylics are made of nylon, and can be left standing in water fairly safely until the end of the painting session. Otherwise, some cleaning of brushes with methylated spirits is possible.

This note of caution aside, acrylics are justly becoming increasingly popular. They combine the advantages of being water-based and quick-drying with many of the facilities of oil paints such as glazing, over-painting, impasto and so on. The ease and speed with which they can be used can give great scope to the visual imagination. Paper of any thickness or weight is suitable: brown wrapping paper, cardboard, canvas of any kind, hardboard, insulation board, stone, metal—even oil-bound surfaces, roughened with sandpaper. Acrylics make a permanent bond with any of these and are said by the factories responsible for developing them to be practically indestructible.

To prime a canvas for acrylics, two or three thin coats of acrylic primer should be applied. Since each coat takes only a few minutes to dry, you do not have to wait long. Emulsion paints are not recommended for use as a primer, even though they are water-bound plastic paints, for they are less strong than paint applied to them. Acrylic primers, being purpose-made, are ideal.

The paint is sold in jars or in tubes. The range of colours is large, and as the medium is developed so the range is extended.

above: **David Hockney** (born 1937)
PICTURE OF A HOLLYWOOD SWIMMING POOL
acrylic on canvas 91 x 122 cm (48 x 36 in)

'In the swimming pool pictures, I had become interested in the more general problems of painting water, finding a way to do it . . . because it can be anything, it can be colour, it's moveable, it has not set visual description.' *David Hockney*, by David Hockney, 1976

below: **Victor Vasarely** (born 1908)
SIKRA oil 170 x 170 cm (67 x 67 in)

A geometrically-based composition. Each part of the regular pattern on the lozenge base board is filled with a challenging shape. Colour plays a dominant part, especially in movement, causing the eye never to be at rest. It is difficult to appreciate this work when seen so small. This was painted before acrylics were freely available. It would have made an ideal subject for the medium.

Extending the drying time

Paint straight from the tube is likely to be too thick to apply without mixing it with water. It is possible to buy a flowing type of paint which is ideal for flat areas. As the paint dries so quickly it is not advisable to squeeze large amounts out of the tube. A liquid retarder is available for slowing down the drying rate, but even using this, the speed of drying still forces the artist to be economical and therefore decisive. Glass is an ideal material for a palette, or a plastic fridge box, lined with damp blotting paper, which is then covered with a sheet of greaseproof paper onto which the paints are squeezed. Since the paints dry out so quickly most makers supply a spare replacement cap of plastic as unless the nozzles are wiped clean each time a tube is used, the metal caps will not screw back on properly.

Acrylic paint dries a similar colour to that when wet. It does not change colour with age, or become more transparent, unlike oil paint. To produce transparent glazes, it is well to use a gel medium instead of water, which will help the paint to retain its acrylic properties.

Three-dimensional works of art

The binding properties of polymer medium makes it ideal for mixing with substances such as sand, pumice and plaster, giving it extra body and thickness. Such materials do, however, wear brushes out quickly. They can, of course, be applied with a palette knife, or any brush no longer in a fit condition for anything else. Relief paintings can be created with such mixtures.

Hard-edge or crisp line paintings are easier to achieve with acrylics than any other medium. Onto the prepared surface masking tape is applied. This tape can be bought at any good hardware or decorator's shop. It is rubbed down firmly on to the surface. Now, by carefully painting up to the edge of the tape and a little over it, letting the paint dry hard before removing the tape, a crisp edge will be left. All paint tends to crack if the tape is pulled away too vigorously, so be careful that the paint is not too thick on the masking tape. This process can be repeated over and over again. The tape can be cut, too, as well as being made to turn in large circles. Sometimes it seems as if acrylic paint is favoured principally for this possibility it offers of making crisp lines!

Acrylic paints have not really been exploited as much as they might be. It took about a hundred years of painting in oils for artists to start really utilizing their potential. Changes happen much more rapidly today, so it is somewhat surprising that painters seem reluctant to use acrylics other than for hard-edge, non-figurative work. The way is open for a revolution in painting methods and techniques, and acrylic paint and polymer media could well be at its start! It is a pity to see such a potentially superb medium so often being treated in the manner of a household decorator's emulsion.

WATERCOLOURS

The use of watercolours is considered by some Europeans to be typically British. However, painters such as Cézanne, Dufy and, earlier, Dürer, worked with watercolour. It is an excellent medium that requires no more in the way of equipment than pans of paint, brushes, clean water, paper and curiosity to produce exciting results.

above left: **T. W. Ward**, *SEA PIECE* (detail)

A less traditional but nevertheless masterly approach; the artist appears to use white pigment in a tint as well as applied direct. The overall result is slightly less than brilliant colour.

above right: **Jean Clark**, *SUFFOLK LANDSCAPE* (detail)

A light, delicate and free way of handling the medium, painted on to grey paper. **A** *dry brush* **B** *hard edge—the paint has been allowed to flood to the edge* **C** *wet paper softens the pigment.*

It differs from other media in that lighter tones are made by dilution, rather than adding white pigment. Light tones are made by white being reflected from the surface of the paper through the thin layers of pigment. The classical way of painting in watercolours is to use no white pigment at all, so that the paint appears to be very nearly transparent. The result is of bright, saturated colour. Watercolour paint can never be made to appear as dark or as brilliant as oil-bound media.

British conventions abandoned

Other forms of water-suspended paints used by artists are gouache, poster colour, acrylic and polymer. Designers' colour or gouache can be used in conjunction with transparent watercolours, although purists might disapprove, conventional British watercolours being painted with transparent or semi-transparent pigment alone. Actually, any mix is satisfactory—with ink, acrylic or chalk—so long as it is permanent enough for the task in hand.

Giving advice about a palette or range of colours for the painter to begin with is always difficult. It is simpler in many ways to have a limited palette. The larger the range of colours in the palette the more freedom you have to decide the range for a particular painting. Over-mixing of pigments can often be the result of too little knowledge of the colours at one's disposal, and produces muddy and flat effects. It is probably best to have an extensive range of colours but to use only a few in any one painting until you have got to know them, widening the range in later paintings.

Your colour range

A colour range for working with landscapes in Britain might be light red, burnt sienna, raw sienna, yellow

William Blake (1757–1824)
BEATRICE ON THE CAR, MATILDA AND DANTE
Pen, pencil and water-colour 24.7 x 35.1 cm ($9\frac{3}{4}$ x $13\frac{3}{4}$ in)

The colour in this illustration, though delightful, is not of prime importance. What is important is the figures, drawn with pen and pencil. The quality of line is both sensitive and deliberate. The images are often symbols: for instance, the leaves have no botanical foundation and water does really not flow in lines.

ochre, cobalt, French ultramarine, crimson lake, gamboge and cadmium orange. So as not to be too disappointed by your first attempts with watercolours, spend some time at home trying out the possibilities of your palette: what happens when you mix one colour with another, what one colour is like when painted over another and so on. With nine pigments it is, theoretically, possible to obtain over 360,000 hues. Some colours will have brilliant results when mixed together while others will be disastrous—but continue to experiment, and try washing out the disasters under the tap, as you may discover something exciting.

Watercolour pigments are solids held in gums. As they dry they become fixed to the surface of the paper. Water evaporates quickly. Once dry the pigments cannot usually be reworked without causing the surface to become blotchy and uneven.

The paints are sold by artists' colourmen in tubes or in pans. Pans come in whole and half sizes.

Palettes are attached to most factory-made paint boxes, but anything non-absorbent that will hold pools or puddles of liquid can be used, from saucers to plastic egg boxes. See also the chapter on oils.

Use two water pots

Water must be kept really clean if you want bright saturated colours; use one water pot for cleaning the brushes and another for mixing paint. A squeezy bottle, such as those that some forms of make-up come in, is ideal for containing water to mix with pigment, but must be cleaned of all oil contamination, as any grease spoils water-bound paints.

One device sold by artists' colourmen is an easel for use out of doors. Though such easels can be a pleasure (and a good thing to drop hints about at present-giving times) they are not absolutely necessary. Instead, make yourself one: a piece of Essex board held against the chest by a strap. The strap should also ensure that the board is tilted at least 20 degrees. The Essex board can be pinned with thumb tacks so that the paper stays flat in the wind.

Watercolour papers. The cost of specially made watercolour papers is prohibitive. It is not necessary to use them for anything other than the traditional type of painting; but again, they make very welcome presents. Since many people will want at least to try them out a description of these papers follows.

The best paper is made from linen and cotton rags. It is nearly indestructible and will therefore outlive many

Stretching paper

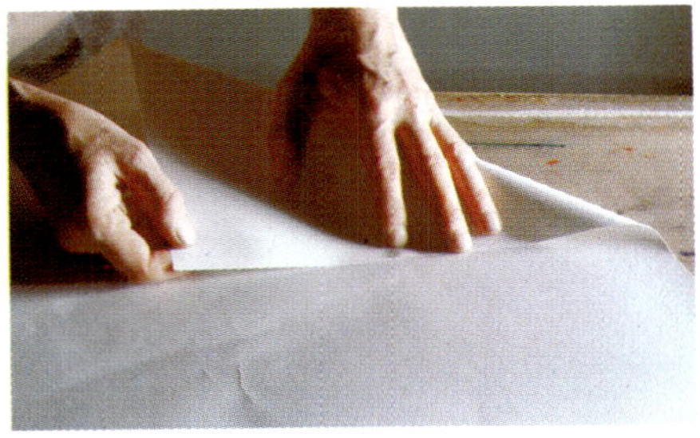

The surface with the less mechanical finish is the correct side to apply paint

Cut all the pieces of gumstrip first—two inches longer than the edges of the paper

Dirty boards stain paper; scrub well with plain water

Wet paper well and wait until it goes quite flat, with no bumps at all—about ten minutes

Stick down long edges first. The paper is still stretching—see bumps on surface: bad workmanship

Rub down gumstrip well, half of it covering the paper. Dry board flat on table or floor

generations of artists. Handmade paper is the most expensive. However, mould-made paper, which is slightly cheaper, is just as delightful to use.

The surfaces of watercolour paper are called NP—not pressed, a naturally bumpy surface, and HP—hot pressed, a finish that makes paper quite smooth. Paper can also be pressed into an artificially rough surface. Each paper manufacturer produces his own range of finishes. One manufacturer's HP, for example, will be smoother than another's.

Try out different kinds

All watercolour paper is treated with size, and different manufacturers use differing quantities. The best way to find out which papers suit which uses is to try out an assortment—small samples can sometimes be obtained.

Essentially, papers are made with two different internal structures: laid and wove. It is fairly easy to tell the difference between them. If laid paper is held up to the light, it is possible to see fine lines running either vertically or horizontally across the surface. These lines are the 'watermark' of a typical piece of laid paper. Laid is stronger than wove paper, and has a more prominent directional grain. Wove papers expand fairly evenly if soaked in water; laid paper expands considerably more in one direction than in another.

Stretching paper is considered necessary if the paper is not fairly heavy, under 140g/m². Wet, unstretched paper cockles and bumps. Flat paper is desirable for laying down washes, otherwise the paint pigment falls into the 'valleys'.

Applying washes needs care

A wash in watercolour painting is a layer of water-bound pigment brushed evenly in one direction over the surface of the paper, and is usually applied with a wide sable and ox brush. First of all the board is tilted to 20 degrees, and the brush is loaded with paint. Starting on one side of the area to be painted, draw the loaded brush across the surface. The paint runs down the tilted board and makes a ridge. (Too much paint will make a runnel.) Reload the brush, and working so that the second brush stroke just meets the first, repeat the process, and continue until the area is covered. With a brush that has been dried gently on a rag, lift the surplus paint, being careful not to remove so much that the bottom of the wash appears pale. Learning how to apply a wash is an exercise that needs practice. It is even harder to put a wash inside the space left by a previous wash. When you can do this without leaving a hard edge, you will have mastered the technique of applying washes.

A second wash should not be applied on top of another until the first is bone dry. To produce intense saturated colour, it is wise to start the first wash with well-watered paint. Some waters cause watercolour pigment to granulate, that is, to go spotty. It is a good idea to test the water first, and use distilled water if necessary. Experience of the paints supplied by your merchant in local tap water will give you the information you need.

To remove unwanted colour from the paper can be tricky. Avoid erasers—fresh white breadcrumbs can be a good alternative. For washes, wet a brush with clean

above: **John Sell Cotman** (1782–1842)
THE MARL PIT watercolour 29.5 x 25.7 cm ($11\frac{5}{8}$ x $10\frac{1}{8}$ in)

Cotman shows us in this watercolour how the simple use of two colour ranges—blue and brown—can be most effective, especially when describing autumn. Notice the large blue area in front of the clouds. It is difficult to know what it is, but it adds a sense of space and depth to the picture. Is is possible in this watercolour to feel the texture and quality of the marl, a chalky clay. The pigment was put on in successively heavier and broken washes, which describe well the appearance of a pit dug out by pick and spade.

water and apply to the affected surface, then blot up excess moisture with blotting or tissue paper. Try to avoid scrubbing the surface.

An alternative method to that of stretching paper is to soak it just before using, and as it dries out apply progressively darker and darker pigment, or work with a pen and ink. This way of handling watercolour paint enables the artist to apply it wet on wet.

Rapid sketches

Tinted papers are available and are usually of the laid type. They are excellent for rapid sketching, as they help to sort out darks from lights. If white paint is used it is possible to extend the tonal range.

Japanese paper can be fun, for it is a little like blotting paper and absorbs pigment rather easily. Conté crayon goes well on to Ingres paper, which is good quality paper made in about three dozen tints. It can be tinted with watercolour afterwards.

Some watercolour techniques

Mix plenty of paint before applying a wash. Keep the colour as clean as possible. A small pot might be useful

Note how well loaded the brush needs to be for wash painting. A large ox and sable brush is most useful

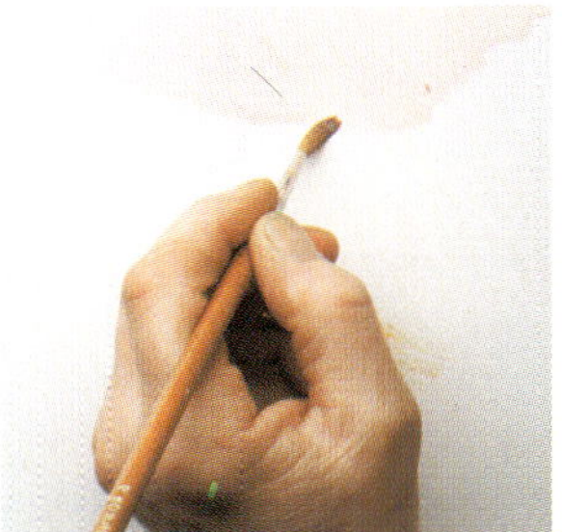

At the bottom of the wash area a puddle may form. It is a help to mop this up with a gentle pinched dry brush

Running up a third colour next to a very wet surface. Note the sensitive way in which the brush is being held

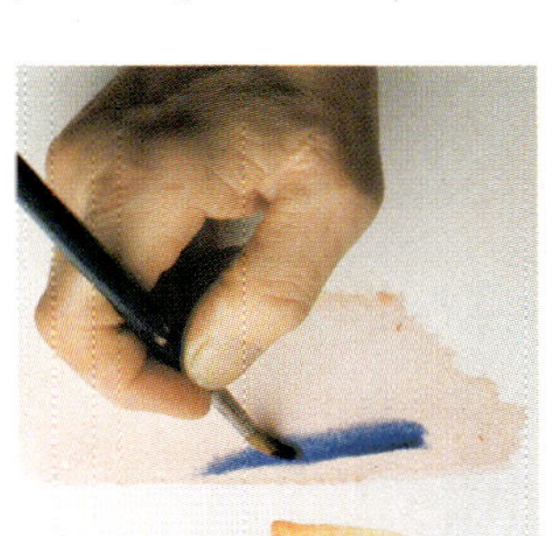

Mixing colours on the paper can cause this mottled effect. If the paper is wet already, the effect is different

A chinese brush makes lively and delicate marks. It is held by poising the hand well above the paper

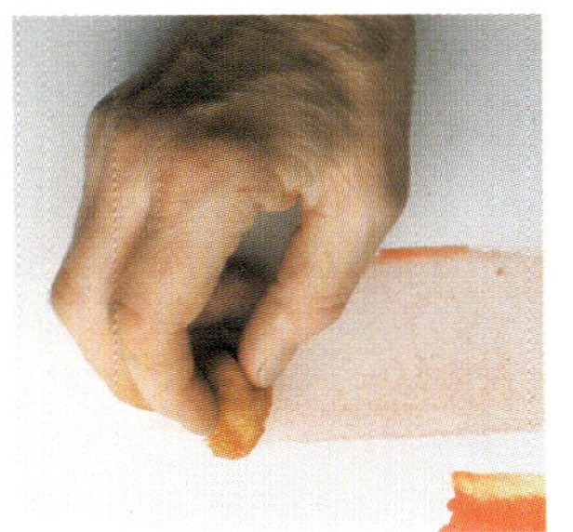

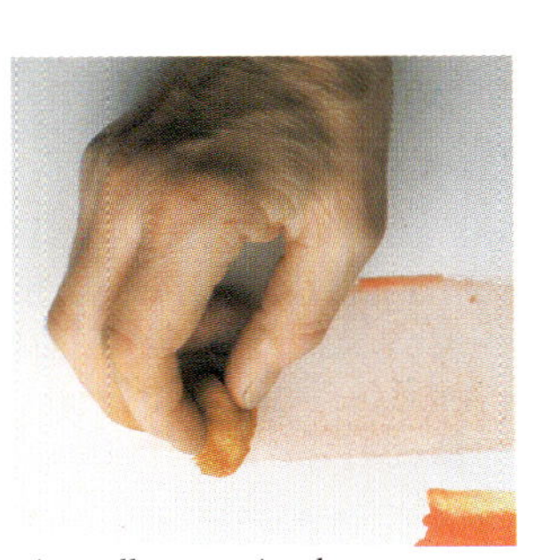

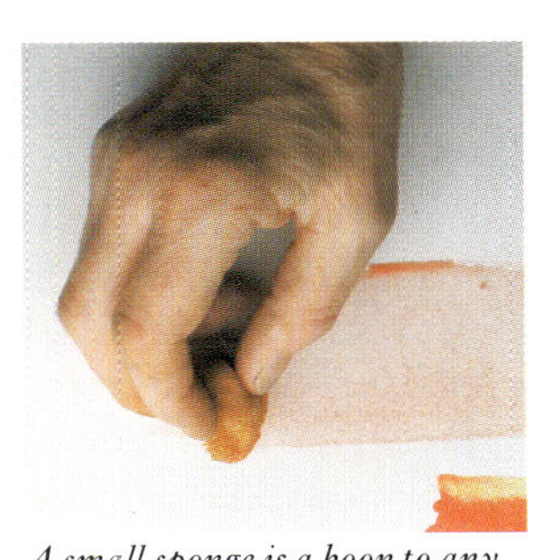

A small sponge is a boon to any artist. Besides being useful for wetting surfaces it is a superb 'paintbrush', ensuring delicacy without finicky detail

Dragging a dry brush across the rough surface of watercolour paper can give helpful results. Try out different levels of wetness and thickness of pigment

MIXED-MEDIA

Art is about exploration and discovery; some artists are frustrated by being limited to a single medium in the making of any one image. They find such a limitation non-productive. Only through combining different media do these artists feel that they are able to exploit and explore their own particular ways of seeing.

With the production of plastic glues, fine quality papers, inks and resins, there is no reason why modern mixed-media paintings should not last as long as the oil paintings of the sixteenth century.

Mixed-media work is probably the cheapest way of making images. Little expertise or purpose-built equipment is required. While craftsmanship is helpful, it is not vital. Most of the tools and materials can be found in any home: scissors, cardboard, magazines and newsprint, fabrics, dyes, candle wax, sticky tape, a single-edged razor blade and a sharp craft knife. PVA adhesive is suitable for most materials that do not have to bear weight, and can be bought fairly cheaply from craft shops.

Needs little physical preparation

A particular advantage of using paper and fabric as picture-making media is that little preparation need be done. Corrugated cardboard, for instance, makes an ideal surface for collage. It can be found outside shops: used packaging material waiting to be collected by dustmen. Sheets one metre square can be commonly found. Such board is stronger than plain card, but if there is any danger of the board warping, it is necessary to paste onto both its sides, with cold-water paste, a sheet of thin paper covering the whole surface. The grain of the paper must flow in the same direction as that of the corrugated card. You can find out the grain direction of paper by laying it on the edge of a table, allowing about 10 cm (4 in) overhang. Then turn it so that the paper lies the opposite way, again allowing 10 cm to overhang. In one instance the paper will droop more than in the other, because the grain of the paper is running in the same direction as the edge of the table. If the grains are not all running the same way, the board will develop a violent twist when it dries.

Techniques that can be applied to surfaces include frottage and collage. Frottage is the making of patterns or textures through rubbing. Any surface that has a prominent, firm, texture can be used—grained wood, concrete, cast-iron coal-holes, shells, the bark of trees. Place a lightweight or soft paper over the textured surface and rub it with a medium such as wax crayon.

Collage is the painterly application of printed textures such as newsprint, magazine pictures, photocopies, photographs, letters or any other ready-made texture or colour. Montage is a similar use of ready-made images.

Mixed-media paintings are often three-dimensional. The varying thickness of paper will provide some surface relief. This quality can be developed further using plaster of Paris, combined with collage and frottage. Other materials can be added such as knitting, string or fur. Plaster can also be drawn on with Indian ink, paint or dyes.

Plaster of Paris can be bought from any builders' merchant. It is very important to mix only a very little at one time, as it sets quickly especially if tepid water is used. Into a smooth flexible plastic bowl put a little cold water—100 cc ($\frac{1}{4}$pt) at most. Scatter dry plaster into the water until it will absorb no more. Always wait until this point before stirring, or the plaster will be difficult to mix. Now stir the water and plaster together with a metal spoon. After a few moments the mixture will be ready, the thickness of double cream. At this stage it can be poured into a prepared mould or allowed to set for about 10 minutes and then worked on to a surface in the same way as quick-setting icing. Note, once the plaster has started to become crystalline or stiff, it should not be worked any more. Once mixed, try not to mix again. If the plaster is to be applied direct to a surface, give that surface a rough texture so that the plaster of Paris can grip it. New additions of plaster will not readily stick to already set plaster, but a coat of PVA will help.

Cleaning

Let the old unused plaster go really hard in the plastic bowl. Then push the sides of the bowl in, and all the old plaster will break away. Never try to scrape it out with a knife, or soak away with water.

New plaster is as heavy as the water with which it was made. It takes several days to dry out; until then it may fall off its support. Cardboard may not be strong enough for plaster, especially if it is applied direct. Try using chipboard instead. Once set, plaster can be cut away, painted, incised or carved.

Although the images made with mixed media may be created direct from a subject matter such as the figure, flowers or still life, they can of course be created entirely from the imagination. Once again, there is no limitation to the simplicity or complexity of the images, though just because the unconventionality of the media might seem to be satisfying enough, composition, structure and space will need especially careful consideration.

Richard Hamilton
(born 1922)
JUST WHAT IS IT THAT MAKES TODAY'S HOMES SO DIFFERENT, SO APPEALING? collage
26 x 25 cm ($10\frac{1}{4}$ x $9\frac{3}{4}$ in)

At first sight this picture might look like a tinted photograph, though on closer inspection it is obviously not. It is a montage painting or collage full of culture symbols of the 1960s, so the scale of the images is directly related to their importance to American and Western society at the time. Much of the success of this work is in the skill with which images were cut out and put together as well as the wit behind the statements.

Raoul Hausmann
(1886–1971)
THE ART CRITIC
photo montage
31.7 x 25.4 cm ($12\frac{1}{2}$ x $9\frac{1}{2}$ in)

Despite the fact this is an anti-establishment piece of art, the current feeling for good taste is evident. To add to its credibility: the letter-forms are in vogue and are spaced well apart, and the colouring is pleasant as well as subdued. Inside the head of the critic is a boot to aid this cultural bovver boy. His pencil has become a sword stick. He has been stabbed by the money he earns. The whole has been assembled with great precision; it is a good drawing.

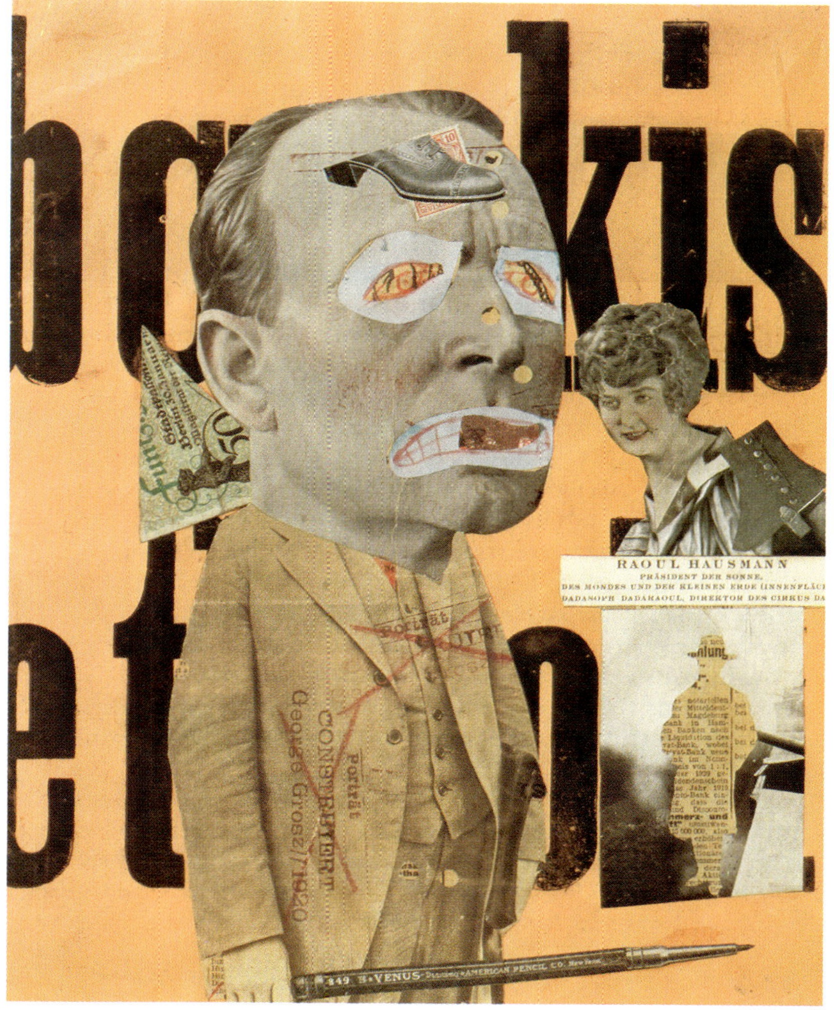

Buying MATERIALS AND EQUIPMENT

Choosing the right artists' materials need not be a difficult task even for the complete beginner. Nor need it be expensive, especially if one is able to attend an art school that has its own materials store. Equipment, though inclined to be costly, will give many years of enjoyment if well looked after.

above: *Few specialist artists' colourmen are still to be found. Such shops can assist the artist in selecting the appropriate materials, with an expertise no general store can ever hope to provide. Their survival depends much on their staff's friendliness and ability to give sound advice to both amateur and professional artist.*

Basic, ready-made equipment, such as brushes, easels and boards, are much the same as they have been since artists' colourmen first manufactured them. Even the materials they are made with have not changed much over the years.

Artists' suppliers and colourmen have two basic desires: to provide the customers with what they want, and at the same time to provide themselves with sufficient money to make the venture worthwhile. Most specialist artists' suppliers spend a considerable amount of time giving helpful advice to both novice and well-established artist. They also have to stock thousands of items, some of which are wanted only very infrequently. They need to charge well in return for this excellent service. The more one buys from a particular store, the happier the salespeople should be to help and suggest cheaper or better alternatives. Chain stores usually charge much the same as the specialists but are unable to give the same knowledgeable service.

Pencils These are sold in two grades: good-quality ones, which are marked with a grading—6B, 5B, 4B, 3B, 2B, B, HB, H, 2H, 3H, 4H, 5H, 6H—and downright awful pencils, which are ungraded and change lead hardness at every stroke. HB is medium hardness, 6B is very soft, and 6H is extremely hard, suitable really only for use on tracing paper, which wears down lead pencils very quickly. It is useful to have a small piece of fine sandpaper available to sharpen the lead of the pencil. A good-quality pencil sharpener is fine, but cheap pencil sharpeners often spell disaster to the artist. Carpenters have special broad, soft, pencils which have many uses—a 'must' if you can find one.

Paper A description of the properties of different papers is given in the chapter on watercolours. For drawing, cartridge paper is most often used, which is usually expensive, so newsprint and layout paper are often good alternatives. If possible choose a paper with a biting surface. This will give textural quality to any line made with pencil, charcoal or crayon. Stocks of coloured papers are sometimes difficult to come by; your local wallpaper shop may let you have some old sample books for a few pence.

Rubbers and erasers Erasers are sold in a large variety of shapes, sizes and colours. The best way of discovering their uses is to try them out. Putty rubbers are useful for charcoal and pastel work. They can be squeezed into points for dabbing off excess pigment. The skid marks on paper from ordinary rubbers may be caused by grease from fingers. It is usually better to leave a line showing than to wear away the surface of the paper by erasing.

Coloured pencils These are lovely to use, and are also sold in a variety of grades. Each trade name, such as Derwent or Verithin, uses consistent hardness throughout the range. Some, such as Conté, can be used as watercolour pencils: applied and wetted with a brush they dissolve. These are not a substitute for tubes or pans of watercolour; watercolour pencils have a quality of their own.

Charcoal Sold in packets of thick, thin or a mixture of the two, charcoal is ideal for quick sketches, life drawings or any marks of deliberate and free quality. It must be fixed with 'fixative' or it will smudge onto other work. Charcoal is also sold encased in wood, as a pencil, or processed as sticks. These are usually more consistent in texture and quality than unprocessed charcoal willow.

Conté crayons (trade name) These are sold individually or in boxes. They are sticks about 100 mm long and 5 mm square of compressed pigment. White, red, brown and black are the usual colours supplied. They also come in varying degrees of hardness.

Pastels Another form of compressed pigment; the range of colours is much wider than with Conté. Again, these are supplied in varying degrees of hardness, each name representing a different degree of 'give'. Pastels are bound in oil or gum. Oil pastels have particularly interesting properties if drawn onto paper soaked in white spirit.

Inks Most inks are waterproof and permanent. Artists' inks dry to a slightly glossy surface and can be diluted with distilled water.

Non-waterproof inks are available mainly for using in reservoir pens. All inks should be shaken well before use.

Black Indian ink is available from Winsor and Newton showrooms in stick form. Ideal for carrying ink around for sketching.

Dip pens with steel nibs are cheap, and excellent. Available with a wide variety of nibs for both illustration and lettering.

Fountain pens Ideal for an individual quality of line, varying in pressure according to the pressure applied. They can only be used with non-waterproof inks, a small range of coloured fountain pen inks are available.

Stylo, Rapidograph or similar pens. These are used by precision draughtsmen–engineers. They do not allow for individuality of the artist's hand, and are not normally recommended for fine art draughtsmen.

Fibre and felt tips In the last few years, pens with fibre tips have become available in a large variety of colours, thickness of nib and grades of hardness. The broad felt tips are ideal for the advertisement artist or visualizer, and fibre tips do have their uses, mostly for the graphic artist. Nearly all are horribly expensive, and dry out quickly. Some use water-based inks and can be washed out, whereas spirit-based inks are permanent.

Sable brushes are the most expensive and luxurious of all. They are all hand-made with carefully graded hair. Sable hair has the supreme advantage that it is naturally curved. The hairs are lined up in the brush so that it always returns to its pointed shape. Sable brushes enable the artist to feel the surface being painted on, as if it were the tips of his fingers carrying the paint. Although they are expensive, they are a joy to use for most media, including oils and acrylics, but especially watercolour and inks. The more liquid the medium, the finer the quality of brush required. Price is usually directly related to quality and size. The blunt ends of the cheaper sable are ideal for oil-bound pigments. Sable brushes are made in a wide range of sizes and shapes, from tiny round ones with hair 5 mm long to large flat wash brushes, which are usually reinforced with ox hair for extra springiness. Cosmetic sable brushes are fairly cheap and can be a good substitute.

Squirrel-hair brushes are soft and have little or no response to the painting surface. They are inexpensive, however, and can be useful for wash or sky surfaces.

Bristle brushes are used for oil painting and for acrylics. The best are hog's hair and are made with naturally flagged ends of the hair using the natural curve. Cheap bristles are ground down to shape. Nylon or synthetic bristle brushes are good substitutes for bristle brushes. These are recommended for acrylics: they are not affected by the medium to the same extent as natural hair or bristle.

Oil and acrylic painting brushes are sold in a variety of shapes—round, oval, flat or filbert, with long or short hairs. Long bristles are needed for rich, thick impasto work, short bristles for precise, sharp touches. One painter said, 'Long bristles put paint on, short ones scrub it off.'

Palette and painting knives An alternative means of applying pigment: painting knives are specially designed for this purpose, while palette knives are sturdier, for mixing paint, but can be used as painting knives. Both are made from smooth flexible steel and come in a wide range of shapes.

Paints and pigments These are written about in the appropriate chapters. It is worth shopping around for paints, as they are not all the same. The consistency and colours of manufacturers' ranges vary from one to another.

Palettes As sold by artists' colourmen, these are usually a waste of money. A quick cheap form of palette is a block of brown craft paper—high quality wrapping paper—held together with a bulldog clip. Each binding medium needs its own palette and is written about in the appropriate chapter.

Canvas The name given to fabrics used as surfaces for oil and acrylic media. Details about how to prepare them are given in the chapter on oil painting (page 38).

Stretchers These are frames used for supporting canvas and can be bought from any good artists' materials supplier; see the chapter on oil painting (page 38).

Easels Expensive, but essential pieces of apparatus if working with oil-bound and acrylic media. Before buying an easel it is sensible to try some out in an art school. Each kind has its disadvantages and advantages.

Drawing boards A wood shop will be happy to supply block board to any size you require. It is possible to buy it as thin as 8mm or $\frac{3}{8}$ in. Its sides need to be finished off with sandpaper. Thin boards may need bracing with two strips of planed wood, 5 mm ($\frac{1}{4}$ in) by 50 mm (20 in) on the back. Block board can be used as a good substitute for specially made boards, which are surprisingly expensive to buy. A useful size board is A1 (92 x 64 cm/36 x 25$\frac{1}{2}$ in) as this is a metric size in which much paper is now being sold.

Pigments These can be bought loose or in tins, ready for mixing as a powder with a binding medium. It is as well to add medium to pigment (in that order) as they can be tricky to mix even with a palette knife. Powder pigments need to be combined with gum or another binding medium otherwise they do not stay stuck to the painted surface.

Medium Glue, gum, egg, oil or varnish can all be used for binding pigments. Each has its appropriate diluent or thinner, whether turpentine, white spirit or water.

Sticky tapes Gum strip is essential when stretching

An easel that you might make

To construct a basic easel prepare wood to the sizes shown below. The back support leg C is connected to the cross bar D with a tee hinge. With coach bolts connect A and B to cross bar D. To make front legs stable, bolt on E which has been glued to F. This unit acts as a variable height support for the picture. To the back of A & B and front of C insert cup hooks 450mm from the floor. Connect together with a light chain or nylon string approximately 1400mm long.

A: 75 × 25 × 1755mm, drill 5mm countersunk bolt holes centred as shown on drawing of easel. Cut angles at foot and round at top.
B: This is mirror image of A. It is desirable to drill both A and B at the same time as A by clamping together face to face.
C: 75 × 25 × 1790mm, (35mm longer than A and B), cut foot at angles shown and round at top.
D: 75 × 25 × 450mm, drill 5mm bolt holes 280 apart.
E: 75 × 25 × 900mm
F: 65 × 35 × 900mm, glue E and F together and drill 5mm bolt holes 25mm apart. See drawing.
***Bolts:** 2 top bolts 5 × 65mm, 2 lower bolts 5 × 100mm, all four fitted with washers and large wingnuts.*
***Tee Hinge:** 250mm, attached with 20mm screws.*

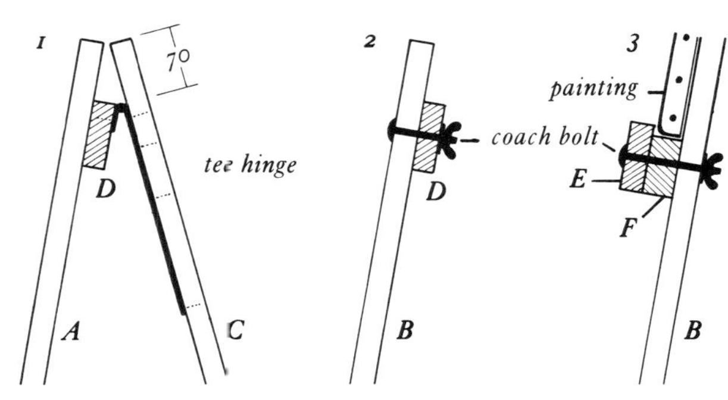

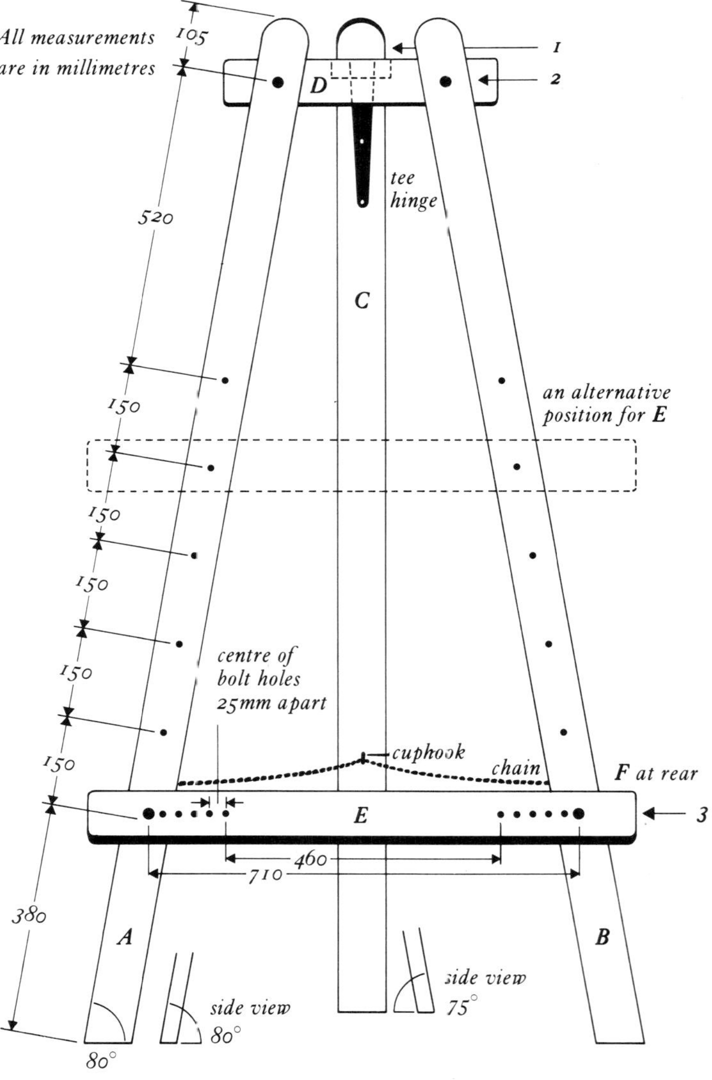

paper. This is the type of sticky tape that needs to be wetted. Be careful to keep the roll away from liquids. Masking tape, as its name suggests, is used for masking out large areas on acrylic and air brush paintings.

Masking fluid Normally used in conjunction with airbrush work, it can also be used as a water-resist with watercolours and mixed-media painting. It is brushed on, and when the painted surface is dry, gently peeled away. Wax has similar properties, but it is less easy to remove afterwards.

Stencils These can be made to one's own design out of stencil paper. It is necessary to use a stipple or toothbrush as the stiff bristles do not work the paint very easily underneath the surface of the stencil paper.

Knives Part of the artist-craftsman's basic equipment; both a scalpel and a Stanley knife are recommended. They both have replaceable blades—blunt knives are useless—and must be used with great caution. Always be aware that the hand that supports the cutting edge needs to be protected in case the blade slips. Gentle pressure is safer than brute force.

Cutting edge For the mounting and cutting up of board and paper it is advisable to use a purpose-made cutting edge, which stops the knife slipping too easily.

Cutting mats Made of plastic and rather expensive, these can be used over and over again, as they are self-sealing. They are helpful to the artist in a variety of tasks.

Stretcher tongs An invaluable piece of equipment for holding the canvas steady and tight when it is being stretched over a frame or stretcher.

Adhesives This is a major subject in itself. As suggested in the chapter on mixed media, PVA adhesive, which is water-soluble until it dries, is absolutely necessary for collage and similar work. For sticking card, UHU is clean and dries quickly, far better than balsa cement. Cow gum, which is a petroleum-based rubber product, is good for paper, handled with care. It should be applied thinly and evenly to both surfaces, and allowed to dry until it has lost its gloss all over. The surfaces once stuck together will not easily come apart. The addition of a piece of clean, ungummed paper placed between the two gummed surfaces and then withdrawn once the correct positioning has been found, can sometimes make the process easier. This is an especially good method of sticking tissue paper. You can buy a cow-gum spreader for a few pence. Adhesives are supplied in spray cans. These are expensive and contain potentially dangerous fumes.

Artists' colourmen make a large range of materials and equipment. Some of the best equipment is often discovered or made by oneself, usually at a fraction of the ready-made cost.

Ultimately, you can save money by improvising and by making use of scrap materials or items of building equipment, but do not skimp on the quality of paints, pigments and brushes.

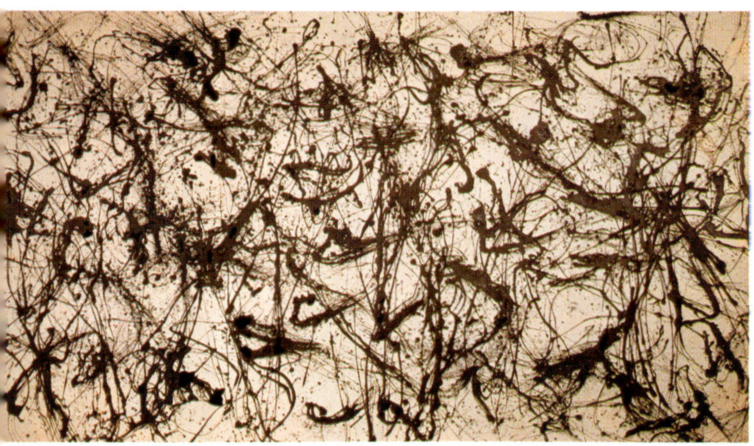

above: **Jackson Pollock** (1912–1956)
NO. 32 oil on canvas 27.6 x 39.6 cm (105¾ x 183⅜ in)

'Abstract painting is abstract. It confronts you. There was a reviewer a while back who wrote that my pictures didn't have any beginning or end. He didn't mean it as a compliment, but it was.' *New Yorker*, 1950

below: **Paul Klee** (1979–1940)
A TINY TALE OF A TINY DWARF
mixed-media

This painting is a doodle, a dreamlike scratching of a pen on the surface of the pigment. Its image has grown according to its own laws, and the artist has suppressed any mental control he might have wished to exercise. The colour is treated in a similar way.

The artist's NOTEBOOK

The sketchbook is the artist's name for his visual notebook. The marks placed in it may serve many purposes. They might be used to explain or sort out an image, to act as a reminder of something seen, or just to jot down a passing thought or image with no purpose in mind for it. Usually, however, sketchbooks contain information which the artist believes will be of direct use to him in the near or distant future.

A sketch might take a few minutes or several hours to make, and is not just a piece of work rushed off without a care in the world with no confrontation or observation. Similarly, the word 'rough' is frequently used by artists for any visual that is not the final work. To rough or sketch-in means laying out in broad terms or making a visual that explains the intention of the artist to a client or patron. Neither 'rough' nor 'sketch' implies, in this context, inaccuracy. On the contrary, a rough is usually the bones of a work-to-be, to give both the artist and potential buyer an idea of its intended finished state. It needs to be accurate as to colour, composition, facts and intention, but never finicky or cramped in manner.

Sketchbooks, like working drawings, usually show more than do finished works about the way knowledge and ideas are come by.

Secret understanding

All too often people say, 'I know what I want to say but I can't find the right words to say it.' The sketchbook is the artist's answer to this dilemma. It allows for risk-taking, encouraging marks that may mean little to anyone other than their author, but which once put down can be explored for their potential. Sketchbooks are private books, revealing the innermost ideas and expressions of visual thought which need to remain nebulous until stated in concrete form.

Once the risk has been taken and images put into the

above left: **Rembrandt van Rijn** (1606–1669)
COURTYARD OF A FARMHOUSE pen and bistre, wash
16.4 x 22.6 cm (6½ x 8⅞ in)

Curious as always about light, Rembrandt is exploring both the effect of cast shadows in an enclosed space, and the way the vine grows up the side of the house and over the wooden slats of the porch roof.

above right: **Leonardo da Vinci** (1452–1519)
HEAD AND SHOULDERS OF A WOMAN
silver point on pink prepared paper 23.2 x 19.1 cm (9⅛ x 7½ in)

Swift studies that helped Leonardo to see how the head, neck and shoulders all fit together. Silver point is a difficult medium, for the marks take some time to darken by oxidization.

above: **Paloma Scott** (born 1957)
SHEET OF STUDIES (detail)
oil pastel on paper 40.7 x 26.5 cm (16 x $10\frac{1}{2}$ in)

This study into Adam's architecture was part of a series of exploratory drawings. While each image was drawn from actual buildings, the artist has made the sheet into one whole decorative element. The information gained in these sketches was found to be insufficient for the artist's needs. Further studies had to be made.

sketchbook, it is easier to see if they are 'reasonable' concepts, and to develop them further in one's chosen medium.

Art students sometimes keep a loose-leaf binder of various papers to use as a sketchbook: some white, some coloured, none of them precious or expensive, but all usable as drawing paper. Both the quality of the paper and the fact that it is unbound helps to stop it seeming 'valuable'. A sketch produced on brown wrapping paper is just as useful as one on super white cartridge; the quality of the insight and investigation does not alter according to the paper you use. I suggest you make such a sketchbook for yourself. A stout piece of card, a bulldog clip and a piece of elastic to hold the paper down in the wind makes an ideal foundation. Use any type of paper and mark-maker you can find; this is also a good way of learning about different media on different surfaces.

above: **Leonardo da Vinci** (1452–1519)
DELUGE black chalk, and brown and yellow inks
16.2 x 20.3 cm ($6\frac{3}{8}$ x 8 in)

By treating forces as solid matter, Leonardo has explored the nature of the impact that is made by falling rocks and flying debris.

Breaking the rules will help

Throughout this book I have stressed in strong terms that detail can ruin drawings and paintings, throwing the work out of proportion. All such rules can be broken at will in the sketchbook. Detail is information, which needs to be expressed and only later discarded if necessary when seen in relationship to the other images in a more finished piece of work.

Comparatively rarely do painters make a single drawing which they can then take back to their studio and turn into a finished painting. Usually they do a series of studies, each one examining a different feature of the subject, which they use as basis for a work in oils, acrylics or mixed media. If for instance the subject matter was the seashore, several drawings might be made of the different states of the tide, the colours of the rocks in and out of the water, shapes of waves under different weather conditions, how the sand changes surface shape, the cloud formations that occur and the shape and colour of the sun at different times. All of these studies would contain a mass of detail and information for future reference. Back in the studio, a preliminary rough might be made, putting the elements into place. The artist might also at some point put the studies away and work entirely from memory. In both instances the artist would filter out information and detail that did not help the painting 'come across'.

FLOWERS

Flowers and plants are symbols of love, peace and purity as well as a potent source of superstition and useful medicine. Each flower has its own unique qualities of shape, size and colour. Delicacy and charm grow alongside strength and robustness, and while some flowers seem everlasting, others bloom only for a few short hours.

Charles Demuth (1883–1935)
RED POPPIES watercolour 35.6 x 50.8 cm (14 x 20 in)
The artist has, like a photographer, moved close in to the subject with his 'viewfinder' so as to cut away from the sides of a possible picture. The result is a taut use of space. The edge of this painting has become an important element in the composition. Botanical accuracy and detail is combined with a modern painterly technique.

Among the most admired of all flower paintings are those of the Dutch. They were and still are major suppliers of seeds and bulbs, and they needed meticulous and colourful catalogue illustrations for their salesmen to carry with them when visiting merchants overseas. Their paintings capture a sensuous response to the beauty of the flowers; sometimes even the nose is deceived into believing the fragrance of the bloom to be captured in the pigment itself. Botanical accuracy and fine detail were an essential ingredient for the Dutch 'catalogue' paintings, but there is of course no absolute need for such precision today.

Remember that flowers are in themselves beautiful, so let the intrinsic quality of the bloom speak for itself.

For the beginner, an excellent medium for flower painting is watercolour; it is clean and direct. The spontaneous manner in which it is used makes it most suitable for a subject matter that changes shape and colour quickly. For your first painting try using heavy-quality watercolour paper, or cartridge. Soak it well with water, drain and place right side up on a clean drawing board. Start by putting in only the colour shapes. Resist the temptation to paint a line and fill it in. Work from one spot outwards, feeling your way to the shape you want. Use well-pigmented colour for this form of painting. While the paper remains wet, the colours will tend to fuse, a point to remember as you paint one mass of pigment close to another.

The space around the flowers

Most people have a potted plant of which they are fond and it will have been put in a place where it looks good. This familiar setting will make an ideal subject for your first flower painting.

As always, you should start with the broad mass of the subject, working up to the fine detail if you so desire. Part of the appeal of flowers is in their massed effect and their scent, and to capture their essential qualities it is necessary to explore their atmospheric space.

Allow the way one colour sits next to another to determine the space and atmosphere of the plant in its environment.

Cover the white surface of the paper as quickly as possible. Only when the paper is covered with pigment will the colours have their true working relationship. A narrow gap of white around a colour can 'lift' and intensify it, as if the sun were shining through the petals or leaves—but this is a trick that should be used deliberately and sparingly.

Odilon Redon (1840–1916)
BOUQUET OF ANEMONES pastel 65 x 63 cm ($25\frac{1}{2}$ x $24\frac{3}{4}$ in)

A direct study that has turned into dream-like fantasy. The vase and flowers have become a single image, surrounded by the aura of colour which seems to fill the volume of space even beyond the picture area.

Confident and bold

Consider from the outset the source of light. Ask yourself whether it is direct, scattered, intense, subdued, coming from behind or in front. The quality of light will change the intensity of the colours and shapes.

As the paper dries out it will be able to take more and more detail. Of course, while the surface is wet with paint you should not work on it too much. Exactly how this will affect your painting will only be discovered through trial and error.

It is a good idea to try and make the personality of the plant recognizable. A rose should obviously be drawn to look as if it is different from an iris. Plants are usually deceptively strong; it is quite common to see grass growing through concrete. Try and exploit the nature of the plant or flower visually. Ask yourself how much, if at all, the flower's colour hides or camouflages such strength. Some plants in the tropics for instance evolve bright and delicate colours so as to be attractive to the animal life they snare.

Try to see each bloom as being like a miniature landscape not just a generalized idea of a flower. A chrysanthemum might be seen to be a little jungle, a primula has the qualities of rolling slopes and valleys. Explore the inside of each flower for its shape and structure as thoroughly as its exterior.

To discover more about the structure of plants it is a good idea to draw, rather than paint, them. Explore the growth patterns through a monochrome medium such as ink or pencil. Either hold in your hand or place next to you a single stem of a flower. Notice particularly the way parts grow out of each other, and the shape that occurs as they become one. See as well the composition of the leaf and petal. Feel them gently between your fingers. Are they soft and fleshy or firm and delicate?

Look and draw decisively. A slow stuttering line is all very well, but try to make a sweeping, sensitive, yet confident line. If the line goes in the wrong place, draw another in the right place. Keep making drawings until you feel you have understood the flower's form and shape. A soft pencil sharpened to a fine chisel point used without undue pressure and a slight turning of the wrist will enable you to draw lines of varying thickness. A wide line is not necessarily a darker line, but has a better chance of inherent rhythm. Dark lines in drawings appear to come forwards; remember this when trying to show petals or leaves in front of each other—again, a trick to be used with discretion.

If you like, try exploring flowers through the media of oils, acrylics or collage. Flowers and plants are an ideal way of finding out how each medium will present its own difficulties, as well as giving its particular satisfaction in a way that no other medium possibly can.

STILL LIFE

The French for 'still life' is '*nature morte*', or 'dead nature', which is an apt description of the subject matter as painted by some artists for their 'five-finger' exercises. A good still life can be as dramatic and poetical as any study of the sea or the nude. Still life painting is worth tackling, but should always be done with vigour and visual curiosity.

One reason for the many uninteresting still life paintings pouring out of art schools every year is the way in which they are set up. Once assembled, they seem to sit around week after week, gathering dust. The only aspect that changes is the fresh quality it had when it was first arranged.

Still life is often chosen as a subject because it does not alter colour quickly or change shape. The longer objects hang around, the more laboured becomes the student's approach until his mind is as stale as the still life.

left: **Henri Fantin-Latour** (1836–1904)
CORNER OF A TABLE oil on canvas
97.2 x 125.1 cm ($38\frac{1}{4}$ x $49\frac{1}{4}$ in)

The artist succeeds in his intention of describing the well-being and comfort of the professional middle classes. Compositionally unusual: the large dark area on the left is well balanced by the flowers in the foreground. The texture of the plant plays up the smoothness of the laundered linen. The slightly horizontal texture of the wallpaper adds stillness to the scene.

equipment for the British landscape artist. Conditions do not stay stable for long enough to set up an easel and the other studio equipment. Watercolours and acrylics are very useful as they are handy and light as well as being set up without too much trouble. Both encourage quick decisions without the need for a great deal of media preparation.

Two essentials to take with you are a strong-handled box to hold your materials, and a strong stool or seat for sitting on that is also the right height from the ground to use as a support for water pots.

Judge the situation afresh each time

British landscapes are rarely painted sufficiently bright and colourful. A useful palette could be: burnt sienna, prussian blue, yellow ochre, and light red. As speed of decision-making is important, a large colour range can make for muddle. As experience is gained, so will the range of colours that will be of use to you expand. People who use exactly the same colour scheme in each painting are not judging the situation afresh each time.

Among the many preconceptions people have about landscapes are that the sky is always blue, earth brown and trees green. Fields, for instance, are an assortment of hundreds of different greens, blues, browns, greys, yellows and reds. One of the artist's tasks is to give them unity, the feeling that the colours are related and part of the same landscape. This is another good reason for using a limited range of pigments on the palette.

Probably a good way to begin is to divide the picture into two tonal areas. The paper, if tinted, will be a light tone, so mid and dark paint tones can be used. While the tonal range is severely limited, the colour range is as wide as your palette. Only increase the tonal range as and when absolutely necessary. Be careful to avoid painting in the small spots of detail that are tonally different. Try using complementary colours; they will reinforce and enhance each other. Remember that one colour relies on another for its full effect.

Be careful, too, about choosing subject matter that you think will make a good piece of art. Better always to choose a view that will enable your particular fascination with landscape to be investigated with imagination.

Obscuring the view

With a cardboard frame made of two L-shaped pieces of card compose the picture area according to the shape of your sketchbook. Be wary of moving in too close and cutting out the surrounding area: cropping is a photographer's trick. Give yourself foreground, middle ground and distance, yet make the spectator's eye work hard to discover that the composition is so simple. Often the centre or focus of attention is better if it is partly obscured by a tree or similar form than standing proud in isolation. Avoid putting it in the centre. For a balanced composition, try two large masses, counter-balancing each other on opposite sides.

Be naïve, see as if looking for the first time, as you make the painting or drawing. Simplify the forms into basic blocks and cylinders. Rarely are the forms and values in landscapes sufficiently simplified. Use detail only to draw attention.

Draw in the growth forms of trees, bearing in mind all the time rhythm and structure. Make a careful choice of a few typical branches that describe the nature of the natural rhythm in the landscape. Make the viewer aware at least of the species to which the tree belongs.

Clouds are solid forms and obey the laws of perspective and foreshortening in just the same way as trees, which appear smaller as they move towards the horizon. Shadows are also real images and follow the laws of perspective.

Persevere, collect as much information as possible. Later, back in the studio, it can be edited and directed to provide the foundation for one or many personal inventions.

Moy Keightley
(born 1927)
GREEN AND BEIGE LANDSCAPE
pastel, gouache, pencil on paper
18.8 x 14.6 cm ($7\frac{1}{4}$ x $5\frac{5}{8}$ in)

Keightley helps the viewer feel the hilly nature of this landscape Houses and trees shelter in the valleys of the hills. It is not difficult to see how the sturdy hedges on the left of the farm track would protect the farmer from wind and rain as he and his family make their way to and from their home.

Painting and drawing the figure has always presented itself as the supreme challenge. The figure, clothed or unclothed, has been an inspiration to artists for thousands of years. Through painting and drawing the figure we explore visual complexities of beings similar to ourselves, presenting problems that appear to stay surprisingly fresh, no matter how often they are seen.

Balthus (born 1908)
THE TURKISH ROOM oil on canvas
179.7 x 210.2 cm ($70\frac{3}{4}$ x $82\frac{3}{4}$ in)

It is a figure painting and a painting of a room and a still life. Everywhere is a point of focus. Space is both pattern and depth.

In the representation of the human body we recognize shapes similar to our own, as well as physical signals that indicate recognizable moods and mannerisms. We are able through experience to read into the slightest of body movements thousands of different shades of meaning. Because we each own a body and live with it for twenty-four hours a day, we believe that we know the shape and colouring of the human figure, though if we look hard at ourselves, and at other people, the idea of an average human shape soon disappears.

Trying to see the whole

Sorting out the minor personal details from the broad

left: **François Boucher** (1703–1770)
LOUISE O'MORPHY oil on canvas
57.8 x 71.3 cm ($22\frac{3}{4}$ x $28\frac{1}{8}$ in)
This arose out of a study for a painting of a girl swimming. Its visual success depends on the velvet environment and tactile trappings of the drawing room, next to colouring of the girl's skin.

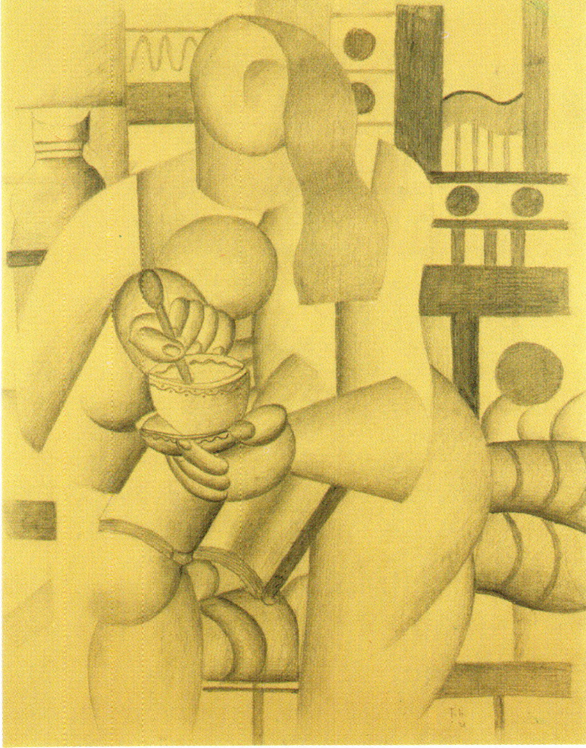

above: **Fernand Léger** (1881–1955)
STUDY FOR LE GRAND DEJEUNER pencil on paper
48.8 x 36.5 cm (19 x $14\frac{1}{4}$ in)

This figure is seen in simple geometric forms. It's solidity is shown through shading. When it suits the artist he ignores his own rules—the hair which is not in shadow is tonally grey. The direction of surface marks indicates the underlying shape. Léger was fascinated by the appearance and function of his present day motor car.

essential elements of the body is a difficult discipline. In a drawing, the colour of the hair, for instance, is usually far less important than the shape of the hair on the head.

The figure is a collection of interlocking boxes held upright by subtle muscular control. The trunk, for instance, is essentially two boxes: the hips or pelvis connected by the bones of the spine to the chest. The spine enables the chest to be at a different angle to the pelvis. Inside the head, which is also a box shape, are the organs of balance. The head tilts and turns to ensure that the body stays balanced when upright. One earlobe is always vertically above an ankle bone when the weight of the body is taken mainly on one leg. The size of the head fits seven times into the length of the adult body in classical proportion.

The pelvis is the junction box for the legs and the trunk. Each thigh bone pivots inside the pelvis and is held in place by a set of large muscles. These muscles cover the thigh bone and run down into the knee. They disguise the skeletal form of the pelvis.

The size of the feet

The whole body is supported by the feet, which are approximately half as big again as the hands. They are remarkably strong structures that spring and flex every time the weight of the body is placed upon them. The hand is able to twist and turn as an extension of the arm. One of its many uses is as a means of communication, being able, like the face, to make the finest gestures meaningful. The hand is also strong and flexible. It can, for instance, open bottles with twist caps and perform the finest feats of surgery. The length of the hand covers the greater part of the face. If the arm is dropped vertically down beside the trunk, the wrist normally aligns with the crotch.

Each one of us has different-sized bones and muscles, as well as varying abilities to manipulate them. Added to this, there are differences in colouring, skin types, hair and general appearance and well-being. It is remarkable that we look as similar as we do.

A thorough knowledge of anatomy and physiology is unlikely to make a person superb at drawing or painting the human figure. Neither is it likely that a rough-and-ready understanding can provide sufficient knowledge. In the early stages of drawing the figure it is useful to study one's own body. This is difficult to do unless one looks in a mirror—otherwise the view of oneself is foreshortened and apparently distorted.

Viewing oneself with detachment can be as startling as hearing oneself for the first time on a tape recorder. These first moments are important, for they display the differences between what we believe we remember about ourselves and the image that confronts us in the mirror. An awareness of oneself helps in understanding what to

top left **Paul Cézanne** (1839–1906)
THE BATHERS oil on canvas 22 x 33 cm ($8\frac{1}{2}$ x $12\frac{1}{2}$ in)

An alla prima painting, executed with the minimum of pigment. The defining of the forms of the bathers, sky and trees took place simultaneously: never allowing one to take over the others. The whole work is a counter-balance of rhythms set up by the figures. The rapid brush work conveys the energy of the bathers.

middle left: **Philip Wilson Steer** (1860–1942)
SEATED NUDE oil on canvas 86.4 x 111.3 cm (34 x 44 in)

One of many studies for a painting called 'The Toilet of Venus'. Delicately painted, her pale colouring makes her appear unapproachable. A nice exploratory and investigatory piece of work.

below left: **Rembrandt van Rijn** (1606–1669)
SLEEPING GIRL bistre and wash 245 x 203 cm ($96\frac{1}{2}$ x 80 in)

A calligraphic brush drawing of the artist's wife, a pose he must have seen her take up many times. Full of energy and speed, Rembrandt draws as if he has just seen her for the first time.

look for in others. Examine through touch and sight what your body is capable of doing and what shapes it makes; what restrains movement and where that movement begins; what else is affected when a limb changes shape or position. Feel the stresses of the body both internally and externally through that sense organ the hand.

As anatomical knowledge accumulates, so the artist's ability to suggest instead of stating underlying forms develops. It is necessary to avoid short cuts to depicting the human form. The method is invented and found each time with fresh understanding.

Life models

Too few life-class models are encouraged by artists or tutors to do their best and often are ignored as people. A person who looks after his models has less difficulty in obtaining their help in taking up a pose that is tiring.

The model has to relax and settle into the chosen pose. The inexperienced model tries to stay rigidly in the position indicated and will quickly tire, while the experienced model understands how to relax and keep the essence of the posture. Watch at this time to see what stresses and tensions there are in the pose.

It is now necessary to ask fundamental questions about the figure before you. The assumption here is that it is a standing pose. Whatever sort of pose the model takes up, the questions are similar. First of all, how is the weight distributed, on one or two legs? If possible, take up a similar pose to the model's for a minute or two. Is the model standing absolutely straight or is there a twist in the trunk, however slight? How are the feet placed in

above: **Aristide Maillol** (1861–1944)
STUDY FOR A FEMALE NUDE black chalk on paper
47.9 x 19 cm ($18\frac{7}{8}$ x $7\frac{1}{2}$ in)

This person has an athletic appearance because her head is much too small in relationship to her height, as well as the width of her neck. A sensitive drawing, which gently uses the mechanical nature of the rough surface of the paper. Notice how when one breast is seen full on, how the other is a three-quarter profile. Also the supporting ankle bone is directly below the model's ear and she looks well balanced. This is a fine example of a working drawing for sculpture. The artist has seen and drawn with understanding the solidity of the limbs and the tensions across her abdomen.

relation to the trunk? If the model is supported by a stick, this produces different weight and balance distribution. What about the angle of the head? Is it looking down or up, over the shoulder or straight ahead? All these questions and more can be answered in the space of two or three seconds, with practice. A useful start is visually to catch the restfulness of the model's rhythm and the movement of the pose.

Looking and seeing the whole

If the pose is set up for any length of time, spend a little while walking around the figure. Make mental notes about what you see, especially anything that helps you understand the mass shape and structure. Pretend that it is possible physically to feel the weight and shapes the model is making. Imagine the feel of the tensions in the back and legs.

Having walked round the model and looked to see how the pose can be perceived as simply as possible, start work. The cardboard frame mentioned previously may be useful. It will help plot the pose in its surroundings and act as guidance as to how to use the area of the paper.

With a soft pencil, charcoal or pen, indicate broadly the rhythms of the pose and the surrounding furniture. An early decision needs to be made whether to include part or all of the model. Having plotted the main features of the drawing, the structure and basic composition, these can be changed and moved for quite some time as long as no one part of the drawing becomes finalized.

Energy and vitality is now important, that is, working without labouring or rendering any small part in detail, keeping the whole drawing plastic and movable.

Stand back now and again

Breaking off from looking at the model every few minutes and looking at how the work is proceeding helps considerably in the difficult but necessary task of ensuring that it is being treated as a whole, and that the temptation is being resisted to join a number of fragmentary pieces together. Some artists make a drawing of the pose, then a second, third and fourth. Each drawing develops and explores what the previous drawing had ignored. An alternative method is to start one and then another a little later. Place the two side by side. Each time a problem arises, work on the second drawing or painting, it being easier to work out problems on a piece of paper or canvas that is not to be taken too seriously.

The human body, whatever its race, is a variety of colours. These colours run rhythmically through the surface of the body. The shadow areas will be of complementary coolness, the lighted areas of warm, flesh tints. These areas will contrast and highlight each other, giving the form solidity and strength. If any part of the body is treated piecemeal, it will appear disjointed and unconvincing, as well as fragmentary.

PORTRAITURE

Portraiture is the most patronized of all forms of fine arts. The good portrait painter rarely has difficulty in earning a reasonable living, for people always enjoy looking at themselves, either in a mirror, or as an image created by someone else. The sitter may not always like the result, but he usually finds the experience of being painted a flattering one.

Every face has in it the life story of its owner. One of the tasks of the portrait painter is to unlock this information and reveal it to the spectator. The artist must abstract from the face and the posture of the sitter those features that are especially characteristic.

Start with a self-portrait

An excellent way to start studying portraiture is to paint your own portrait. Set up a mirror in such a way that the light on the canvas is the same as the light falling on yourself. The self-portrait is often the most difficult commission an artist can undertake! Usually the eyes are painted much too large, because of course one stares at oneself throughout the sitting. Despite its difficulty, this exercise is really a 'must' for any aspiring artist.

The placing of the canvas in relation to the sitter is very important. Place the canvas alongside the sitter, and then take a few paces backwards so that both canvas and sitter can be seen at the same time quite clearly. Mark the spot where you stand. The illumination should be as similar as possible for both canvas and model.

Begin by dividing the picture area into light and dark. Observe the shadows cast—the eyes, for example, will almost certainly be in shadow cast by the bones of the brow. Dilute flesh tones well, and paint them in loosely. If you do this on an underlayer of brown, the result will be a cool neutral colouring.

The portrait will now be a generalized statement in two tones, dark and light. Avoid painting in features or details during the early stages. Gradually introduce further tones. Colour need not be limited to the same extent, but do try to keep the painting simple and uncluttered. Only paint what you can define as a shape or area.

Return to the marked spot

At no time check if what you are doing is 'right' in relation to the model while you are standing at the canvas. Always return to the marked spot and observe the two together. In this way it is easier to resist the temptation to touch in small details. Boldness as always is essential. Spend much, much more time observing the model than using your brush. Use large brushes with lots of paint; keep the palette as simple and as limited as possible.

above: **Amedeo Modigliani** (1884–1920)
YOUNG FARMER oil on canvas 73.5 x 50 cm ($28\frac{3}{4}$ x $19\frac{1}{2}$ in)

A painting that might have been done from memory and consequently from imagination. An artist much influenced by the sculptured African tribal art, giving his work a mask-like quality. The violent brush strokes behind the head accentuate the severity of the face which is not filled with unnecessary information.

Gilbert Stuart(1755–1828)
GEORGE WASHINGTON
oil on canvas
71.2 x 49.5 cm (28 x 19½ in)

A superb portrait in the classical manner. It also displays a nice sense of three-dimensionality. The artist has seen the sitter from below, which gives the viewer a feeling of stature. Note the highlight in the eyes and the cast shadow from their lids. The nose also throws a shadow across to the lips, connecting with the dark area on the side of the face. The red background drape enhances the skin complexion and the contrasting green in the shadow areas. The fine frilly jabot is an excellent foil to the smoothness of the face.

Spend a whole hour on the first, that is, the two-tone stage; this is time for composition and design.

The canvas should not be loaded with thick paint at this stage—it is often a sign of having come to conclusions too quickly. The whole session should not be longer than two hours, with frequent breaks for the model to rest.

Be at ease with your sitter. Spend some time with him beforehand in the room in which you intend to paint, for he will feel happier about that you are doing.

Portraits are not to be rushed

The whole portrait may take as many as seven sittings. Each layer of oil paint must be allowed to dry hard before the next session. It is also necessary to ensure continuity not only of lighting but also of background.

Remember that the form of the face is never round; it is rather a series of planes that appear to be rounded. As with figure-drawing, think three-dimensionally, as if you were working in clay, and be aware of the solid areas of space around the head, neck and shoulders.

A few visits to your local art gallery can be of enormous assistance, once you have completed at least one portrait. By looking at other people's work, it is often possible to discover new ways of seeing.

Tonality, or values, is an important compositional consideration. Check the colour and tones of shadows, keep measuring one tone against another, or else some parts will appear to be more in the foreground than others, upsetting the balance of the whole. Remember that short brush strokes blend into each other, which is useful when trying to depict softness.

Do not be worried if a likeness is not achieved immediately. The ability to paint accurate portraits comes from continual observation of people and how different colours, lighting conditions and surroundings affect them. Try out different media. Each one will reveal to you a little more about the art and craft of portraiture.

ABSTRACTING

As we have discovered, each person sees and perceives objects and the environment around him in a way that is particular to himself. We therefore as artists make visuals that highlight the way we perceive, painting and drawing that which is important to us, leaving out or playing down what is to us unimportant. This is the beginning of abstract art.

Kurt Schwitters (1887–1948)
HAIR-NAVEL PICTURE (HERZ PICTURE 21 B)
oil on board with painted relief of wood, cloth, earthenware and hair 91 x 72.5 cm ($35\frac{3}{4}$ x $28\frac{1}{2}$ in)

A pleasant collage of ephemera. An anti-Art object executed with a little pomposity. To us today, too much like Art to be anti-Art.

All painting, drawing and sculpture is a form of abstract art. No work of art depicts the whole of reality, just a small segment. Abstract, or non-figurative art can be considered in a number of ways. First is the kind of work that simplifies and reduces complex visual problems to their minimum and essential details. Mondrian in his early work typifies this approach. His paintings of natural forms such as trees are semi-geometric in their simplicity. The seemingly very abstract patterns of his later works (see page 71) probably derive and are abstracted from the pattern of fields and canals in his Dutch homeland.

The second way is non-representational in origin, a constructivist approach: the building up of images organically. One such artist was Jackson Pollock (page 55) who poured liquid pigment over large canvases, building up complex colour and shape combinations. An alternative constructivist approach is the geometrical. The typical abstract geometrical painter uses large instruments to make exact geometrical relationships.

left: **Willem de Kooning** (born 1904)
PINK ANGELS oil on canvas with charcoal
132.1 x 101.8 cm (52 x 40 in)

The size of this work gives an indication of the considerable energy of the artist. He has made every mark telling, even the dribbles at the base of the canvas. The human figure was the source in this exploratory 'abstract' painting. Each colour and shape nudges and reflects its neighbours.

below: **Piet Mondrian** (1872–1944)
BROADWAY BOOGIE-WOOGIE oil on canvas
127 x 127 cm (50 x 50 in)

A constructed painting, based loosely on geometrical exactness. The colours, I suspect, are placed at intervals that are rhythmic rather than mathematical. Unlike his other paintings it is lean and starved of pigment, but has a sense of mischief and fun.

Challenging convention

A large part of non-figurative art is anti-formal. It is used by artists who are endeavouring to break away from classical ways of depicting objects, situations and people. Non-figurative art can be a forceful way of stimulating vision and perception without producing what have traditionally been recognized as works of art.

Since the turn of the century when man started to develop a more positive approach to the understanding of time and space, the artist has wanted to share in the exploration through his own media. One painter, Duchamp, tried to depict in a painting the continual movement of a nude person walking downstairs. Picasso painted faces in which it is possible to see both the profile and the full face at the same time. These artists abstracted information and put together images in a way not previously seen on canvas.

There is said to be at the moment a movement back to representational art, since artists and students are drawing objects and people as they understand them to look. The process of drawing is being rediscovered as a core activity in exploration and transformation.

The difference between painting, drawing and sculpture is becoming increasingly difficult to define. I suspect that for those who do not find the border blurred it is because they as artists rarely believe they step near the boundary in their own work.

The art of television

Kinetic art, where movement, or the illusion of motion, is the main element, demonstrates some of the difficulty in defining the difference between drawing and sculpture. It explores the inter-relationship of light and time. A typical kinetic art object is a series of lights coming from shiny moving surfaces. A mobile made of pieces of foil would produce this effect. The medium of film and television is also considered kinetic art; sometimes a more painterly art form would be difficult to find. A cine film is a strip of frames containing images that are slightly different from each other. The order or sequence in which these frames are shown is of paramount importance, as is the speed at which the film is projected.

The artist's curiosity about light, time and perception was illustrated in the early 1970s at the Op Art exhibition in London. Paintings that looked like moving sculptures in two dimensions played tricks on our eyes; so powerful was the effect that the security guards wore shades or sunglasses. These geometrical works rely on voluntary, or self-inflicted compulsory participation to become active and real. They use tricks of illusion to make our eyes weep, wonder and not believe what is put in front of them. By placing shapes and colours next to each other, in particular ways, vibrations occur on a grand scale.

Although optical and similar forms of art evolve and quickly disappear, they are in their way important and vital visual stimulants to the fantasies of the artist. It is through such art that the artist hopes to touch the perception of the spectator, playing and working on the association of ideas, as well as time and spatial relationships.

Imagination is necessary for the gap between bisual aspirations, fantasies, and present abilities to be crossed. As long as the gap is not too large, it is usually manageable, especially if the artist is willing to use unconventional means of travel.

Many more people are now able to read and take in images that twenty years ago were incomprehensible.

Wassily Kandinsky (1886–1944)
IMPROVISATION—KLAMM oil on canvas
111.1 x 111.1 cm (43¾ x 43¾ in)

The essence of this artist's work at this stage of his life, is colour and the forces that are created when they are placed next to each other. Each element in this work is deliberate as well as placed with a sense of fun and spontaneity. Activity and zest occur through the liberal mixture of pure, well-saturated colours and restful tints. Although this artist is devoted to non-figurative work he includes a dancing couple two-thirds down the canvas.
'The observer must learn to look at the picture as a graphic representation of a *mood* and not as a representation of *objects.' Kandinsky*

The distorted images of the 1950s and '60s are now more easily understood than at the time they were unveiled. The distortions appear less, the visual vocabulary has become part of our everyday visual language, helped considerably by the advertisements on television and street posters.

The difficulty is that as fast as the images become meaningful and exciting to the public, the artist is leaping ahead with fresh ideas. In the late 1970s a British painter and film-maker, Christopher Welsby, set up a cine camera with the lens pointed towards the sky. Every few seconds an exposure was made (time-lapse), and this went on for 24 hours. The result was a short film shown on a screen like the canvas of a painting: the sky changed colour and shape as the clouds gathered, then rained; became dark during the night and then light again in the morning. The spectators or the film's audience were distressed by the speed and rhythm of the changing images: an unconventional form of painting, but a direct way of grasping at the spectator's perception. This is just one of the many ways painters are exploring the way we perceive.

Now computers can assist the artist

The tools and materials of the non-figurative artist may well be the usual ones of brush, easel and pencil, but many now are turning to the complexities of video and the cathode ray tube. With the introduction of home video machines which include portable cameras, pictures can be made that may be shown instantly on television. They can be linked into a computer—at present rather expensive—to produce sophisticated kinetic art. In the future, these techniques will be within the ability and grasp of anyone who can today afford a TV game. The process is at present experimental. The results achieved may sometimes be accidental, but they still compete for their place next to those images made by artists that are deliberate, planned and scheduled.

Many aspirant artists, fascinated and intrigued by discovering images, are unhappy about using conventional painting media. They delight in making 'pictures' with the aid of mirrors, video, pieces of shiny metal, computers, acrylic sheeting, film, glass, resin, paper, wood and anything else that extends the way they see. While artists want to go on making discoveries, art will never become a dead language. It takes no special qualifications to become an explorer of the visual universe.

Michael Moon (born 1937)
OMEGA acrylic on calico and cotton
167.1 x 213.4 cm ($65\frac{3}{4}$ x $82\frac{7}{8}$ in)

This work, painted in 1979, is a collage. It is about the quality of coloured textures applied to surfaces that are not uniform. The visual impact of the paint on these surfaces is tentative, as well as assertive. The ambiguity of vision is still apparent, but it is no longer concerned with figure and ground, for the two have become one. This artist belongs to one of many different streams of fine art in Britain today.

ART CLASSES

Art schools are places of goodwill, as well as shared experience. For some reason there is something good about watching other people struggling and finding answers to the many problems they are encountering. Learning has a new meaning when the process is pleasurable and the effects obvious. Mistakes are encouraged, even praised, and success is personal rather than competitive.

above: *Etching is a fine way of developing one's drawing skills. An artist's proof being taken.*

Every year, two months before the start of the academic year, thousands of people once again wonder how they are going to use the coming winter evenings. While some of them turn to learning a new language, or music, many others, adventurous in another way, consider studying drawing, painting or a craft. They wish to be creative, and discover something of the personal rewards associated with practising the arts.

Most people have imagination, and those who claim they have none can soon be shown otherwise by any good tutor. Imagination needs nurturing with friendly tutorial advice.

Working with others

The art school environment respects the need for privacy. Those students who do not like asking for assistance are helped by being in company with others who are seeking answers to their dilemmas, learning by observation.

Painting and drawing is hard work, but because it is a satisfying activity people at art school are seldom aware at the time of how much physical and mental energy it uses. Hours slip past, an inner feeling of satisfaction is gained, helped on by watching the excitement of others realizing and seeing for the first time.

In most parts of Britain selecting a school for part-time study is quite easy for most people, as there is only one school nearby, and the fees are amazingly modest in spite of recent increases. For those who have a choice of school, it is a good idea to try and spend some time visiting them to see which one has the most congenial atmosphere. This atmosphere is usually more important than the standard of work on show.

Some classes during bad, or really hot, weather drop in numbers. Such times can be excellent for inquiring if the course has a vacancy. Art classes are popular, and some people stay on from one year to the next. These people usually have first option on any places offered at the start of the session.

Going empty handed but receptive

A question that is often asked is what equipment should be taken to the first art class. This really depends on the purpose of your study. So before considering the equipment question decide what you want out of an evening or two at art school. Many, I suspect, go solely for companionship, and others to learn by being with fellow artists who are tackling the same problems. Some want to learn techniques, and seek continuous guidance and instruction. After a few weeks you will probably be clearer about your aims.

When you have decided which art class to join, talk to the tutor in charge about equipment, telling him of your aspirations. If at first it seems that all is not going as well as you had hoped, try and stick at it for a while, at least one term, and if possible, the whole year. If you are allowed, try out new subjects and processes. Each one will help the others. You should soon discover which are for you.

Taking a break of a week or two

Should you be so unfortunate as to miss several classes, the tutor will be happy to see you again. People have all sorts of reasons for being away, and no one will question you about your absence unless you wish to tell them.

At the end of each year there is always an exhibition of work as well as small displays throughout the year. If what you are doing shows a sense of discovery, it might well be put on show, especially if it is work from a sketchbook.

Full-time courses in art are available to the teenager and the mature student alike. Just as teenagers are most welcome at part-time evening and Saturday art classes, so the older student is an essential ingredient for the rounded full-time vocational or degree course.

In England and Wales, art college full-time courses are divided into three major groups—foundation, degree, or vocational. The foundation year, in which students extend their visual curiosity, is a course that is designed to help the students decide what area of art and design they wish to study for a further period. The idea is not so much to study different techniques, but to examine one's own personal way of seeing. This might indeed be done through such subjects as printmaking and calligraphy.

Subsequent course subjects include fashion, theatre sets and costume design, sculpture, ceramics, and painting—there are about fifteen different subject areas. These higher-level courses are either vocational and career-based, or degree courses and therefore fairly academic. Most higher-level courses prefer students to have completed a foundation course no matter how experienced they might already be.

Grants are generally available for most British full-time courses. Your local education authority and the National Union of Students in London can advise you on the likelihood of your receiving one.

Entry requirements

Entry into full-time courses usually requires an interview. A folio of work is of course the most important aspect of any student's application. A folio at this stage should be full and not selective. Drawings made on scraps of paper on the top of a bus, for example, can be of considerable use to the interviewer. A tidy, well-ordered folio is more helpful than a display of mounted work. A folio that shows a span of work over many years is also desirable but by no means essential.

Exam results are always important, mainly because examining bodies find these a useful guide. Most exams at this level are devised by universities that are unable as yet to understand the difference between learning by doing and learning by thinking. Some grant awards depend on the number of 'O' levels or CSEs a person has obtained. It is better that a student has passed all such examinations before starting a full-time course in art.

Another revealing aspect of an interview is the way the candidate responds to questions about his work. Some foundation courses can afford to be selective and require considerable evidence of dedication to the idea of pursuing the study of art over the coming two, four or five years. The length of study will much depend on the candidate's age, aspirations and abilities. These are sometimes only discovered during the foundation course.

Visual curiosity is all-important

A sketchbook or visual notebook will be of great help to any applicant. Art college staff, especially those teaching on foundation courses, are looking for flexibility and the willingness of a student to put aside hard-and-fast beliefs or preconceptions. The visual notebook is an excellent indicator of the way a person responds to and tackles what he sees. Some people find talking about their work difficult; but the tutor may gain considerable insight into the student's visual and intellectual curiosity by looking at his sketchbook.

Contrary to many people's impressions of life at art school, the working hours are long. A student is expected to work each weekday from 9.30 am to 7.00 or 8.00 pm most evenings. The average college year has 36 weeks. For the keen student, the vacation is another study period. The day is taken up with lectures and practical work. Most degree students are expected to write three or four essays each term.

For anyone who wants to follow art and design as a career, The Design Council, Haymarket, London SW1 has produced two excellent reports on the industry: Carter and Molton. The Society of Industrial Artists and Designers, the professional designers' chartered organization, at 12 Carlton House Terrace, London SW1, is able to assist and advise those who write and ask.

Until recently, the good professional fine artist could, it was considered, always find a teaching post. In exactly the same way as in the other arts subjects, a degree is not a passport to work. Many painters and sculptors have to take on work of a different kind to provide them with a livelihood. It is sometimes through this work that they discover just how necessary it is for them to paint and draw.

EXHIBITING

There are two kinds of exhibitions: the one-person show and the large multi-person show. We are all intrigued to know what others think of our work. It is also good for us to see our work next to others' and for comparisons to be made, however much we may disagree with the opinions expressed. Every one of us has it in us to be our own art critic.

above: *Visitors at an open air exhibition of paintings, drawings, sculpture and pottery. Anybody is allowed to exhibit at this site, professional, amateur or complete beginner.*

Every year during the spring months, immense numbers of paintings and sculptures arrive at the Royal Academy of Arts, Piccadilly, London, for the annual summer show. Out of the many entered, comparatively few are chosen. It is an exhibition open to all: the novice, professional, student and amateur. It is a show seen by thousands, a large percentage of the works are sold, and introductions to new patrons are made. Other open shows include those of the Royal Society of British Artists (RBA) and the Royal Watercolour Society.

Most local art institutes and societies have an annual show in the town hall or public library. This is where most people are able to display their work for the first time. No matter how humble the exhibition, even if it is on the railings of a local park on a Sunday afternoon, the way the work is presented is important. It is probably true to say that if the picture frame is for some reason very noticeable, it is not doing its job well. The frame is there to present the picture, not itself; yet, strangely enough, the smaller the picture, the larger the mount and frame should be in proportion. Sometimes the frame with mount can be as much as three times the size of the drawing or painting enclosed. Large paintings, on the other hand, can be effectively presented in a comparatively narrow frame, or with only a narrow band of wood tacked neatly to the side of the canvas, hiding the unpainted edges.

Making your own frames

Frames can be made from ready-made easy-to-assemble mouldings. For the more adventurous, wooden moulding is sold in lengths which have to be cut to fit. This is a job that requires some skill. The equipment needed is a mitre block, tenon saw, hand drill, small hammer, set square, and a clamp or vice. **1** Measure up the painting, having chosen a moulding that is sympathetic to both the painting and the mount. Add twice the width of moulding to each piece cut to allow for mitring, and also a small margin to allow for the slight expansion or contraction of the painting in varying temperatures. **2** Cut moulding into lengths with a 90-degree or right-angle cut. Make sure that the shorter pieces are the same length, and the longer pieces likewise. **3** Even with a mitre block, a device which holds the saw at 45 degrees, it is difficult to cut mouldings accurately, but it can be done with a little practice and a good tenon saw. **4** Once mitred, clamp together a short and a long side on a bench or table top. **5** Drill, at a slight angle, a fine hole in each side piece so that a pin can be inserted which will help hold the joint together. Repeat for each of the four corners. Number or code each piece so that the parts will fit together again later. **6** Apply a little resin woodworking glue to one surface, put the pieces together, tapping the pins into the holes. To be sure the frame sets square, place a set square firmly inside the inner corner. Clamp the frame tight with G-clamps, string loops or nails in the bench. Once the glue has set hard, lightly hammer the pins with a nail puch so they are fully recessed into the wood.

Glass can be bought cut to size. Always ask for picture glass, which is thinner and clearer than window glass. Glass is used as a protection against dust and the atmosphere, so it is vital for drawings, prints and similar works of art.

Cutting of mounts

Prints and paintings on paper such as watercolours normally need to be mounted. The window mount is usually considered the most satisfactory of all mounting systems. A hole is cut into a sheet of card through which the work is viewed. **1** Select the card. Special mounting boards are available, some of which have coloured surfaces. When a window is cut out of this board it leaves a cream border the thickness of the card. Be wary of coloured board, for it can swamp the drawing or print to be mounted. For a very small drawing, a large mount is probably needed. **2** To determine the size of the card to suit the picture, place the card on the floor, holding the picture in the hands. Move it closer and further away from the board. This will allow you to see the picture larger or smaller in relation to the board. **3** On a sheet of tracing or greaseproof paper, mark the size of the picture. Add 3 mm ($\frac{1}{4}$ in) all round for the bevelled hole in the mount before drawing it out carefully on the greaseproof paper. **4** Place it in the exact position on the right side of the card. If it is a vertical or portrait picture it is usual to allow a little extra space at the bottom. With a pin or needle gently prick a hole in each corner of the proposed window. **5** Place a steel cutting edge on the board so that it joins two of the points. With a brand-new blade in a Stanley knife, hold it so that the bladed surface is at 45 degrees to the face of the board, the point of the blade going into the picture area. With the knife edge towards you, dig the point sharply into the board about 3 mm from the pin prick furthest away from you. Running the knife along the side of the cutting edge, pull the blade towards you. For the blade to cut cleanly, it must be really sharp. This is helped by keeping the blade at an angle, so the cutting edge of the knife is as long as possible. When the blade has reached the pin prick nearest to you, stop. Repeat for all four sides of the window. The cleanest edges are made with one cut. If done perfectly, the middle will drop out; if they do not, extend each cut ensuring that the crispness of the corner bevel is not lost. Any furry edges can be cleaned up with flour glass paper. Cutting well-bevelled mounts takes practice. Straight-sided windows are considerably easier, but do not usually look as good. The bevelled border makes a pleasing step between mount and picture. **6** Fix a piece of plain board the same size to the back of a mount with gum strip. This is done by laying the two next to each other, and when the gum strip is dry, folding the two together to form a hinge. **7** Place the picture in the position that corresponds to the prepared window on to the backing board. **8** Fold a piece of gummed tape to form a 'stamp hinge'. Stick to the underside of the picture at each corner. Replace picture in position and stick down each corner in turn. **9** Now the mounted work is ready to go into its frame, held firmly in place with a sheet of masonite or hardboard. Fix the hardboard in place with small panel pins. Once they are in position, slide the head of the hammer against the board, tap the pins firmly into place in the edge of the frame. **10** Again with gum strip, seal all the gaps at the back firmly and cleanly. The result should be an airproof, mounted and framed picture.

Finally, go to exhibitions and see how other artists mount their work. Make critical assessments and helpful notes for your future reference.

GLOSSARY of terms

Alla prima: completing a picture in one session. Usually a colour rather than a monochrome painting
Bevelled: sloping
Bistre: burnt wood
Brightness: the strength of colour in terms of light and dark
Brilliance: those colours that combine saturation and purity with brightness
Cast shadow: the shadow of an object next to the object that caused it
Chinagraph: a soft waxy pencil that draws on glass or similar shiny surfaces
Chipboard: a composition board made of wood chippings. A very dense material
Colourman: The person who prepares artists' materials, and probably sells them in retail shops
Compounded: intensified or made greater by adding an extra element
Concept: an idea or notion. A visual concept is an image that describes an idea
Diluent: a thinner for a medium, for instance water for gums, turpentine for oils
Encaustic: a technique where wax as a medium is heated with an iron. The wax then becomes part of the material and acts as a resist
Essex board: a proprietary insulation board
Figure/ground: term, from Gestalt psychology, for the shapes on their background. Sometimes the two change place and the figure becomes ground. This is an ambiguity the artist enjoys using. See Composing the picture (page 28)
Filbert: rounded and pointed shape of oil brush
Fixative: a liquid sprayed on to pastel and chalk drawings to stop them smudging
Focus: when images are seen as sharply as possible, or our attention is drawn to a particular point
Foreshortening: an aspect of perspective
Fugitive: a colour that is likely to fade in light or in the atmosphere
Gestalt: the ability to see the whole image from the parts shown. A tendency we all have of jumping to conclusions on the basis of what we see or hear
Gesso: a simple mix of dead plaster of Paris and size. A semi-absorbent painting surface
Glaze: a transparent or semi-transparent layer of paint
Glue: used technically meaning an adhesive that is heated and applied to two surfaces, which under pressure will stick together
Gouache: a refined version of poster paint that is sold in a large selection of colours
Ground: the prepared surface, see Oils (page 38)
Hue: a particular colour found in the visible spectrum. There are said to be 150 discernible differences of hue. The warm colours of red and yellow are divided into more hues than the cool greens, blues and violets at the other end of the spectrum
Highlights: small areas of 'white' or comparatively light tones on an object
Impasto: thickly applied paint (in contrast to glazes)
Landscape: used technically to denote a horizontal rather than vertically shaped picture
Liner: the small flat or bevelled area between the picture and the outer frame
Local colour: the actual colour of objects without taking into account reflected colour of light
Media: plural of medium, the materials rather than the equipment used by the artist: oil, film, ink, television
Medium: singular of media, or the binding liquid mixed with powdered pigment to make paint
Mitre: 45-degree angled cut
Mobile: a piece of work that can freely or fluidly change shape
Modelling: representing three-dimensional form on a two-dimensional surface
Opaque: see opacity
Opacity: not allowing light to be transmitted
Painterly: being directly concerned about areas of colour, tone, texture and light. Resisting the temptation to draw a shape and fill it in
Palette: range of colours; or the surface on which the pigment is mixed before being applied
Paste: used technically to mean an adhesive made with water and cellulose
Pastiche: a work consisting of elements from many other works, a kind of super-forgery. It is a term used in the theatre in describing super-real period stage sets. More in the flavour of the original than the original
Perceive: the way we become aware of our surroundings through our senses, especially sight
Permanent colour: Pigment that is unlikely to fade in sunlight or in various air conditions
Picture plane: the imaginary surface where the space of the picture and that of the viewer meet. It is in the same place as the painting surface of a picture
Portrait: upright picture, see Landscape (page 62)
Projection: a line or shape jutting out. The process of carrying a line or shape onwards.
Relief: three-dimensional surface
Research: ordered and planned investigation, of looking
Resist: a substance such as wax or oil that repels water
Saturation: a purity of colour measured against a similar area of equal brightness that contains no colour
Scumbling: see Oils (page 38)
Spatial: of space
Spectrum: normally thought of as the colours of the rainbow. The range of colours in light
Stippling: dabbing with a hard brush
Straight edge: steel rule used as an edge for cutting
Stretcher: a wooden frame often specially made on which canvas is tacked so as to hold it stable. See Oils (page 39)
Tint: a thinned or whitened version of a hue
Tone: a word used by some artists to mean brightness in colour. Also used to mean light and dark
Turbid medium effect: optical effect of blueness created when a dark colour is partially obscured by a smoky or milky semi-transparent layer of paint
Turpentine: a solvent for oil paint, not to be confused with white spirit which in the fine arts is used mainly as a cleaning agent and behaves differently as a diluent
Values: the observed tone, or light and shade of an object when related to the tone of another object in the same picture area

Video: means of putting on to a magnetic tape visual images in an electronic form. To be viewed the images are put on a television or cathode-ray tube

Viewing frame: two L-shaped pieces of card that allow an artist to compose a picture in much the same way as a viewfinder would be used in a camera

BOOKS that might be helpful

Blake, V. *Art and Craft of Drawing*, London and New York 1975

——— *The Way to Sketch*, Oxford 1929

Bone, S. *Oil Painting*, London 1956

Clark, K. *The Nude*, London and New York 1967

Dorf, B. *Beginner's Guide to Painting in Oils*, Levittown, N.Y., 1972; London 1973

——— *Beginner's Guide to Water-colour Painting*, Levittown, N.Y., 1972; London 1973

Fry, R. *Vision and Design*, London 1937

Gray, N. *Lettering as Drawing*, London and Fairlawn, N.J., 1970

Hayes, C. *Complete Guide to Painting and Drawing Techniques and Materials*, Oxford and New York 1979

Hiler, H. *The Painter's Pocket Book of Methods and Materials*, London 1937

Hyder, M. *Picture Framing*, London 1963

Itten, J. *Art of Colour*, New York and Wokingham 1974

Jameson, K. *Painting, a Complete Guide*, London 1975

Kandinsky, W. *Concerning the Spiritual in Art*, London and New York 1977

Mayer, R. *The Artist's Handbook of Materials and Techniques*, London and New York 1951

Murray, P., and Murray, L. *Dictionary of Art and Artists*, London and New York 1969

Osborne, H. (ed.) *Oxford Companion to Art*, London and New York 1970

Read, H. *Education through Art*, London 1943

Ruhemann, H., and Kemp, E. *The Artist at Work*, London 1950

Stokes, A. *Colour and Form*, London 1950

Richmond, L., and Littlejohns, J. *Fundamentals of Water-colour Painting*, London and New York 1978

Vernon, M. D. *Psychology of Perception*, London and Baltimore, Md, 1970

Watson, L. *Supernature*, London and New York 1974

White, J. *The Birth and Rebirth of Pictorial Space*, 2nd edn, London and New York 1973

ACKNOWLEDGEMENTS

The publishers would like to thank the following: *A.D.A.G.P.*: 12 (above), 66 (top), 68, 71 (below), 72. *The Josef Albers Foundation Inc.*, Orange, Conn.: 11 (above). *Alte Pinakothek*, Munich (Photo J. Blauel): 65 (above). *The Art Institute of Chicago*: 18 (Mr and Mrs Lewis L. Coburn Memorial Collection), 60 (Ada Turnbull Hertle Fund). *The Arts Council of Great Britain*, London: 44 (left), 44 (right), 73. *The Barber Institute of Fine Arts*, The University of Birmingham, England: 19. *Collection Mr and Mrs Irving Berlin*, New Tork, © 1973, Grandma Moses Properties, Inc., NYC: 12 (below). *The British Museum*, London: 47, 66 (below). *David Clark*: 34. *Jean Clark*, Shottisham, Woodbridge, Suffolk: 46 (right). *A. C. Cooper*: 12 (above). *The Cooper-Bridgeman Library*, London: 47, 65 (below), 68 (Private Collection). *Ron Cosford*, London: Jacket, 14 (below), 15 (below), 48, 49. *Adrian Field*, London: 1, 2–3, 4, 5, 11 (below), 39, 41 (below), 52, 63 (reproduced by permission of the artist), 74, 77. *The Fine Arts Museums*, San Francisco: 16 (left). *The Foundation E. G. Bührle Collection*, Zurich: 20 (below). *Geheimes Statsarchiv, Berlin*: 33 (bottom left). *The Hamlyn Group Picture Library*, London: 35, 45 (below) (by kind permission of the artist), 66 (top), 66 (below). *Robert Harding*, London: 31, 32, 55 (above) *Reproduced by Gracious Permission of Her Majesty the Queen*: 33 (top left), 36 (right), 56 (right), 57 (right). *The Hermitage*, Leningrad: 7, 21, 29 (centre). © *D. Hockney* 1964, Courtesy Petersburg Press: 45 (above). *The Imperial War Museum*, London: 29 (top). *Knoedler Gallery*, London 23 (above left). *Kunsthalle*, Tübingen: 57 (above). *Brian Lock*: 54. *The Lord's Gallery*, London, © Cosmopress, Geneva: 70. *Louvre, Paris*: 66 (top). *Helge and Dr Rolf Marti Collection*, Berne: 55 (below). *Photo MAS*, Barcelona: 14 (above), 17, 27 (right), 61. *Musée Bayeux*: 35. *Musée des Beaux-Arts*, Jules Cheret de Nice (Photo Lorenzo): 23 (above right). *Musée National d' Art Moderne*, Centre G. Pompidou, Paris: 64. *Musée Picasso*, Barcelona: 61. *Museo de Arte de Cataluna*, Barcelona: 27 (right). *Museo de Arte Moderno*, Barcelona: 15 (above), 17. *Museum Boymans-van Beuningen*, Rotterdam: 12 (above). *Museum of Fine Arts*, Budapest (foto Alfred Schiller): 56 (left). *The Museum of Modern Art*, New York: 71 (below), 72. *The National Gallery*, London: 4, 38 (above left), 38 (centre left), 38 (centre right), 43. *The National Gallery of Art*, Washington, D.C. (Andrew W. Mellon Collection): 69. *The National Gallery of Victoria*, Melbourne (Felton Bequest 1926): 15 (above). *National Museum Vincent van Gogh*, Amsterdam: 8, 26. *Norwich Castle Museum* (Norfolk Museums Service): 49 (top left). *Petit Palais*, Paris (Photographie Giraudon): 59. *Rijksmuseum*, Amsterdam: 16. *Rijksmuseum Kröller-Müller, Otterlo, Holland*: 65 (below). *Paloma Scott*, © The Central School of Art, London: 57 (below). *Sotheby Parke-Bernet*, New York (E.P.A. Photo): 58. *S.P.A.D.E.M.*: 4, 18, 20 (below), 29 (centre), 23 (top right), 38, 45 (below), 59, 61, 64, 65 (below), 67. *Staatliche Museen Preussischer Kulturbesitz*, Berlin-Dahlem (Photo Bildarchiv Preussischer Kulturbesitz): 37. *Helen Sutherland Collection*: 62. *The Taft Museum*, Cincinnati, Ohio (Louis Taft Semple Bequest): 40. *Tass Photo*: 7, 21, 29 (centre), 33 (bottom right). *The Tate Gallery*, London: 9, 30, 31, 41 (above), 42, 51 (below), 57 (below). *The Victoria and Albert Museum*, London: 29 (below), 67. *T. W. Ward*, Holbrooks, Suffolk: 46 (left). *John Webb*, London: 51 (below). *Frederick Weisman Family Collection*: 71 (above). *The Whitworth Art Gallery*, Manchester University: 33 (centre right). *The Williamson Art Gallery*, Birkenhead: 66 (centre). *Derrick Witty*, London: 9, 31, 34, 38 (centre right), 41 (above), 42, 43, 46 (left), 46 (right), 57 (below).

INDEX

Figures in **bold** type refer to illustrations